WHEN TEARS
LEAVE SCARS

A TRUE STORY OF
TRIUMPH
OVER EMOTIONAL ABUSE

WHEN TEARS LEAVE SCARS

A TRUE STORY OF
TRIUMPH
OVER EMOTIONAL ABUSE

ALLISON K. DAGNEY

WHEN TEARS LEAVE SCARS:
A TRUE STORY OF TRIUMPH OVER EMOTIONAL ABUSE

ISBN: 978-0-578-80921-2

Printed in the United States of America

Find out more at www.whentearsleavescars.com

DISCLAIMER

My memories are imperfect; however, I share these stories to the best of my knowledge, and I have changed identities to stave off legal woes.

This book is dedicated to Claire, Lleyton, and Carter—my precious gifts from God.

You are the reason I never gave up.

And to DC,

You have supported me and given me strength. You've been my light in the darkest nights. You were the soldier who pulled me through the toughest moments of my life. I will forever be grateful to you for your selfless and unconditional acts of love.

TABLE OF CONTENTS

CHAPTER 1

MARRIED – 17 YEARS

've lost count of how many times I've imagined his death. I'm not sure when I started daydreaming about all the possible ways he could die. There were slow agonizing deaths, and quick, almost painless deaths. It didn't really matter in the end. How he died wasn't as important as that he died.

I always heard when people become severely depressed they spiral into such darkness that suicide is the only way out. The pain is so unbearable and death is their only escape. For me, it wasn't the same. I yearned to live, and I wanted him to die instead. I wished and prayed for it. I prayed to God his SUV would tumble into the creek, running parallel to the country road leading him home from his six-figure job. But, always to my disappointment, my husband still walked through the door every evening after work, donning his suit and tie.

Images and fantasies of his stiff, dead body on our marriage bed swirled in my mind. Thoughts him vanishing from my life like an apparition fading into the darkness became my obsession. I didn't want to die. I wanted him to die; crashing his car, falling off a ladder, getting hit by a bus. I wanted him to die and it didn't matter how.

I imagined his funeral in my daydreams. His shiny, black casket at the head of the church and me feeling the burning urge to vomit, listening to his family and friends murmur softly about how wonderful he was. I replayed the fantasy in my mind of his brothers lowering the heavy coffin carefully onto the steel rails above a hole that wouldn't bring him close enough to hell. Hurry it up you guys. Get this over with.

I had considered killing him myself, but there was one major flaw with this idea: I am not a killer. I didn't know if I could actually hurt him, let alone kill him. Could I live with the consequences? Could I live with myself? Just understanding why I wanted him to die was difficult for me. Sadness, frustration, confusion, and defeat plagued me. All I knew was that he was not the same person I married and he made my life a living hell.

How would I explain it to the police? My family? My children? Could I get away with it? I knew without a shadow of a doubt I couldn't live my life this way any longer. There had to be a way out. I couldn't deal with the pain and confusion. The constant criticism and guilt trips were unbearable. The sneaky manipulation of my emotions and oppressive control of my every move had me backed into a corner like a scared animal ready to attack. I recognized something was very wrong, but I couldn't pinpoint the nagging ache that made me feel so alone—lost and on the brink of losing myself forever.

Before Nick came home from work that evening, I removed my loaded, chambered handgun from its locked vault. I held it for a few minutes and ran my fingertips over the black gunmetal. I thought about what it would be like to kill him and how simple it would be to squeeze the trigger while I fearfully admired the weapon. I quickly put the vision out of my mind, shook it off of my thoughts like a dirty washcloth and placed the gun in the safe. I locked it in the nightstand and slid the key under the mattress.

It was our anniversary, and yet, I wanted nothing more than for my husband to be dead. He planned a dinner out and though I had no interest in being with him to celebrate a lifetime of heartache, sadness, and fear, I complied as always.

"Are you almost ready to go?" Nick yelled from the living room as I was slipping into my little, red sundress. The sound of his throaty voice scraped at my eardrums.

"Almost," I yelled, in unison with him slamming the door.

Nick hated to wait. I looked at myself in the mirror, swept my dark hair behind my neck, grabbed my heels, slung my purse over my shoulder, and rushed out to the empty living room. The dark reflection of myself in the oversized flat screen TV stalled me. All of the colors in the image of myself were muted. It was me, but it wasn't. A marked sadness behind my hazel eyes, and a deep crevice of concern held steady like a vertical scar between my brows. I rubbed the wrinkle with my forefinger in a futile attempt to iron it out.

Nick's horn blared from the garage and I was startled from my daze. My spine stiffened. I sprinted barefoot from the living room to his car. He sighed heavily and shook his head as I tossed myself inside, buckled my seatbelt, and fumbled to put on my shoes.

"I'm sorry," I huffed.

"I told you I wanted to leave at 6."

"It's 6:03." I smiled and pointed to the clock on the dashboard.

"Exactly, you're late."

"Three minutes!" I snapped back.

"Just goes to show your lack of respect for me. You'd think you would be more considerate for our anniversary date. I got the kids to my mom's so you could have plenty of time to get ready. I planned this entire thing for you and you can't even be ready on time."

He sounded so formal, professional, and sterile.

"You're really wearing *that*?" he asked, looking me up and down like I had leprosy.

Nick wore khaki shorts and a faded, hand-me-down polo shirt from his brother.

"You think I overdressed?" I asked.

"I never said that."

Self-conscious of my attire but afraid to ask to change, I kept silent to avoid more conflict. Nick wouldn't want to waste more time for me to change my clothes. Nick would want me to deal with it. So I did. I always did what Nick wanted.

I flipped the visor down and applied my lip-gloss in the mirror. He flipped it back up.

"What the hell is your problem?!" I yelled.

"Allison! Don't use cuss words with me. Only stupid people cuss because they're not smart enough to come up with better words."

This wasn't getting off to a very good start. I screwed the cap on my gloss and jammed it in my purse as he pulled out of the driveway. My emotions would be suppressed to avoid further upsetting him. I stared straight ahead, unmoving.

"Sorry," I said.

I lowered my eyes and stared at my smooth-shaven knees peeking from under the red, floral printed cotton. The tone was set for the night. I would have rather stayed home.

My hope was that we would have a nice time. I always had hope. I reflected back to when we first dated and how much fun we had together. He doted on me, he complimented me, and he treated me like a princess. But years had passed since then and I thought maybe all marriages ended up like this over time.

Neither of us spoke as we drove to the restaurant in silence. After parking, we crossed the cobblestone street toward the small dining establishment he had picked. Nick walked briskly ahead of me; I walked faster to keep up with him, careful not to lock one of my heels in the uneven pavement. When we reached the restaurant, Nick held the door for another couple coming in, and then me.

"This place is nice," I said as I gazed around the room.

It was dimly lit with small tea light lamps and the tables were neatly dressed in crisp linens. The faint clanking of silverware and dishes from the kitchen echoed through the dining area. The aroma of charred steak danced under my nostrils. A pretty young hostess directed us to our table. I had put on my best dress, best smile, and best attitude for the night. I would be careful not to say something to upset or annoy my husband. I watched him study the menu.

"What are you getting?" I asked.

Nick's eyes inspected his options while I eagerly anticipated hearing what he would order.

"I think I'll get the 5-ounce filet. That sounds good," he said.

The price of his meal was $27.99. Ordering something of a higher price than my husband would be too risky. Without even perusing the menu, I decided to order the same meal as my husband.

"I'll have the steak too," I said.

"Why do you always get the same thing I get?" he asked, crinkling his brows.

"I don't. Do I?"

"You do. And it's weird," he laughed. "So, next time, I'm going to make you order first."

His eyes darted around as he studied my face.

"What? Do I have something on my face?"

I reached around to grab my purse from the back of the chair, but he stopped me.

"You look really pretty tonight. That's all."

"Oh, thank you."

An unexpected compliment. It made me feel really good. I smiled.

The rest of our anniversary date was uneventful. We stuffed ourselves full of so much food and drinks and we opted to go straight home and skip dessert. On the drive home, Nick told me to write a letter to the restaurant management telling them about how awful our experience was. I objected.

"But it wasn't awful. It was great."

"Why do you have to argue with me on everything? Just write them the letter and tell them how disappointed we were in the food and the service. They'll write us back and offer us a gift card or a free meal to come back to make it right."

"That's really wrong. That's dishonest."

"First of all, I've told you before not to give me your opinion unless I ask for it. You're making a big deal of nothing. Why do you act so weird?"

"I don't want to do that. You can do it if you want to, but I don't like it. It's not right."

"You don't like it? It's not right? You're the only person who thinks like that."

He rolled his eyes in disapproval of me. I was silent. *Who is this man?* I knew in my gut this was wrong. He was wrong.

"You know, you act so holier-than-thou. Act like you've never used a coupon in your life or gotten something for free. What kind of person judges someone but does the same exact thing? I hope God forgives you. I really do. This is not the kind of person you really want to be. This isn't who I want my wife to be."

An immediate urge to jump out of the car rushed over me. I stared at the door handle wondering if I could do it. *He hopes God forgives me? Who the hell talks to their wife like this?* My face was burning hot with rage. Thoughts of what to say to him wrestled in my mind. *Who the hell do you think you are? You're an asshole. I hate you. Why don't you just die?!* Instead, I choked down my words, sat there in silence, stone-faced, clinging to fantasies of my dead husband.

That night, after we both settled into bed, Nick laid asleep facing away from me. I was sure he was deep in dreams for about thirty minutes by his heavy breathing and light snore. I rolled over as slowly as I could trying not to wake him and reached for my handgun. The bedroom was black, but my fingers knew exactly where to find it. The bullet was prepared to explode from the barrel. It waited patiently for my finger's command. All I had to do was pull the trigger.

Cautiously, I pulled myself up to my knees, quietly and slowly making sure not to move the mattress with my movements. The gun was heavier than I remembered as I raised it carefully in Nick's direction. My heart pounding like a drum in my chest and I drew in tiny breaths of air and expelled them out even slower. Nick could wake at the slightest sound or movement. It was imperative I take my time, regardless of how quickly I wanted to get it over with. *Slow. Slowly.*

I aimed the gun at the back of his head imagining the blood pouring from his skull onto the freshly cleaned pillowcase. *Stop shaking. Steady.* My mind amplified everything. My senses were heightened. The sounds of my breath were roaring. The quivering of my hands on the pistol was erratic. Yet, somehow, Nick was silent, perfectly still. I steadily touched my index finger to the trigger and squeezed my eyes shut tightly. My heart pumped faster as I attempted to control my breathing. *Calm down Allie. Hold yourself together.* Memories of my life shuffled before me. The whirlwind of love with Nick: our wedding, buying our first home, and the joy of the births of our children. *How can it be I so badly want to rid this man of my life, of his life? Could I be so cold-hearted to murder him in his sleep, in our bed? How easy would it be to end it all?* I held every ounce of power and he was completely defenseless. All I had to do was shoot and it would all be over.

Instantly, my entire body shook, causing me to lose my grip on the gun. It descended clumsily onto the bed making no sound as it landed. It was as if gravity took it from me. Suddenly, my upper body felt like a powerful snake was constricting me and there was no room for air in my lungs. Sucking in as hard as I could for oxygen sent me into a panic. The tears uncontrollably dripped out of my eyelids.

"Allie? Are you okay? Wake up." Nick interrupted my sleep, yanking me out of a nightmare I wasn't completely sure I wanted to escape. "You had a bad dream."

My emotions were bursting out of me like a broken dam. My body was tingling from head to toe. I couldn't breathe and I was gasping for air. Nick sat up, switched on his bed lamp, and slid his thick glasses onto his nose.

"You're having an anxiety attack," he said.

"I. . .can't . . .breathe. . ." I said between sharp sucks of air.

"Calm down. What's wrong with you? Take slow breaths. You're fine. Just calm down and breathe. Everything's fine."

The weight of the world was resting on my chest. The tears wouldn't stop. There wasn't enough air. I was trembling and my face was soaked. *God, make it stop, please.* I cried and heaved for what seemed like an eternity. Nick looked on like I was crazy with little empathy, annoyed by me waking him and waiting for the attack to end.

After my panic subsided, he reached up to switch off the lamp and flopped to his pillow. The dream was so real. Part of me was relieved it wasn't, yet the other part wished it had been. The dream was more real than any daytime fantasy I'd conjured; I ran to the bathroom and vomited up my sin.

CHAPTER 2

MEETING NICK AND DATING – 1 MONTH

Nick and I met on a blind date. He was 18 and I was 19. He was seeing multiple girls, while I was single and looking for a relationship. The night we were set up, I walked into the freshman dorm room with my friend, Sasha, to meet him. The room smelled of stale beer and dirty spaghetti bowls. The living area was filled with lots of people I didn't know and empty red, Solo® cups cluttered the tables and countertops. In the corner sofa, an attractive, voluptuous girl was draped like a blanket over an average looking guy. She laughed at his jokes and they flirted like they were newly dating.

"That's him over there by the window," Sasha said, pointing right at the couple on the couch.

Well this ought to be interesting, I shot her a wide-eyed smirk.

"Did you tell him we were coming?" I whispered, surprised by the audacity of his inconsideration.

"Yeah." She shrugged and bounced off with one of Nick's fraternity brothers. I walked over to him and introduced myself, shoving my hand out in front of me, annoyed.

"I'm Allie."

As he stood up, I tilted my head back to keep our eyes locked. The girl on his lap hopped off abruptly and rolled her eyes as she walked away. He wore an Abercrombie and Fitch t-shirt and cargo shorts. A braided hemp and steel necklace clutched his neck. He was well-groomed and his sandy, blonde hair was styled. He wasn't overly handsome, but good looking nonetheless. His nose and chin were strong, and his brown eyes were warm. He was lean, muscular, and mildly attractive. He took my hand and shook it firmly. His hand was soft and warm.

"I'm Nick," he told me, flashing a big white smile and looking directly into my eyes.

"Sorry about that," he apologized as he nodded toward the rejected sorority girl. He set his sights on me, studying my face. Slight insecurity brushed over me. There was an awkward silence. I interrupted the pause and broke eye contact, looking over at my friend.

"So, Sasha said we're going golfing. Are you any good?" I asked.

"By golfing, do you mean driving around in a golf cart and drinking beer?"

We both laughed. Nick seemed to have a good sense of humor. He was well-spoken, polite, charming, chivalrous, and intelligent. He was fun to be with, and it was clear he was liked by the people who knew him. His popularity among the fraternities and sororities was glaring. He was all-around impressive, and I knew within days of meeting him that I wanted to be his girlfriend.

After the first date went well, we had a second and then a third. I was falling hard for Nick. Our next three weeks together were a rapid romantic progression. It came to my attention through a friend that Nick was still talking to other girls while we were dating. My intention was to be exclusive with him, so I put my foot down and told him if he wanted to be with me, he would need to drop every other girl he was seeing. He seemed surprised by this, but he quickly obliged.

By month one, we had already expressed we loved each other and were exclusively boyfriend and girlfriend. We were intensely involved and spent all of our free time together. We snuck off to be alone whenever we could, and his hands were magnets for my body. I was giddy and my heart raced just being near him. I shared intimate details about my life with him—my fears and dreams and my insecurities. I felt safe with him and there was closeness with Nick I'd never felt before.

One sunny afternoon Nick and I lay lazily on a hammock in his parents' backyard. My cheek rested on his bare chest. His heart pulsed lightly in my ear. I wanted to spend every minute of my life with him. Dreams of a wedding, children, and happily ever after were stuck on repeat in my mind. Nick spoiled me. He bought me piles of gifts: clothes, shoes, flowers, jewelry, and concert tickets. He took me on romantic dates and did thoughtful gestures. Nick said I was his soul mate and he wanted to spend the rest of his life with me. I couldn't believe I had found the love of my life.

"Your birthday's coming up," I drew my finger along his collarbone, "what do you want me to get you?"

Nick would be turning 19 in a week. Gifts were fun and I enjoyed giving them. I couldn't wait to celebrate his birthday.

"I don't want you to get me anything. You're my gift." He kissed me gently on the head. His skin was warm on my face.

"But I really want to do something nice for you. There has to be something you want. Come on. There has to be at least one thing."

"Well, if you really want to—" he hesitated.

"Yes! Please, tell me!" As I sat up quickly, I sent the hammock rocking unsteadily and we both almost tumbled out onto the grass. I squealed and we erupted in laughter.

"Okay, okay." His laughter dissolved and we steadied ourselves. "One thing I'd really love from you is for you not to wear any makeup on my birthday."

My excitement was stifled, and the mood changed quickly. The muscles behind my eyebrows constricted tightly. *Did he just say what I think he said?*

"What? Why? That's weird."

My face twisted in confusion as I tried to figure out why he would want me barefaced as a birthday present.

"It's definitely not weird. I don't want any material gifts from you. If I want something, I'll buy it myself. I have money. If I want something, I'll just buy it. I want a meaningful gift, something special no one else can do for me. I would always prefer acts of kindness over something you can buy at a store."

It sounded lovely and I tossed the idea in my head. I was still unnerved. Wearing no makeup made me very uncomfortable. Call it a crutch, call it fake, call it whatever you want. Ultimately, I didn't go without makeup in public and that was that.

"No," I moaned. "That's not a gift. That's not what I meant."

"You are more beautiful with no makeup on and you want to make me happy don't you? You asked me what I wanted and that's the only thing I want."

"I know, but it doesn't make me happy at all."

"Well, you asked me what I wanted for my birthday. I guess I was assuming this was about me, and not you."

His eyelids grew heavy and he slowly turned his head away from me. Sensing his disappointment, I quickly adjusted my stance.

"No, no. I mean, yes! It is your birthday. I just wanted to get you a gift, that's all."

Backtracking my selfishness was embarrassing. *I shouldn't have said anything.* Explaining to Nick how I felt ugly, vulnerable, and exposed was the only thing I could do.

"Allie, you are beautiful naturally. You don't need makeup! I promise! Look at your perfect little nose and your pretty, heart-shaped lips."

He kissed his index finger and drew a line down the bridge of my nose and pressed it to my lips.

"And your hazel eyes," he said admiringly, staring deep into my soul. "They are the prettiest eyes I've ever seen." The sweetness in his words made my heart flutter and my cheeks ruddy.

I was worried about what others would think of me and what he would think of me. After digesting what he said, it did seem like such a simple thing to do. His happiness was important to me, so I did what he wanted.

The next week at his rather large family party, I walked in with a sheepish look on my face in place of make-up. The pride in Nick's eyes was enough to lessen my discomfort. My sacrifice, little as it was, made him beam.

I was introduced to aunts, uncles, and cousins. There were so many people. His family was much larger and extended than my own. Keeping track of new names was overwhelming. Everyone had brought a gift except me. I arrived empty-handed and barefaced, embarrassed to say the least. But it seemed like Nick was pleased. He was happy. This was strange for me, but still slightly soothing at the same time. I'd done what he wanted, and he was happy. The rest of the family seemed to accept my gift to him without the blink of an eye.

Blinded by my love for him, I was unable to see the truth behind this sacrifice. In just a few weeks into a very green relationship with a stranger, me giving in to his subtle request was a test, and I passed it with flying colors. Although I couldn't perceive it as such, it led Nick to realize, if I was willing to do *that* for him, I'd be willing to do anything he wanted.

CHAPTER 3

DATING – 6 MONTHS

"Allie! Can you come here for a second?" Nick yelled from the laundry room of his parents' house.

I jumped up from the living room sofa and hurried to see what help I could give.

"Can you help me sort out all of this laundry?"

Sitting on the floor before us were two big baskets of Nick's dirty clothes. His mom and dad were in San Diego on vacation while Nick, his brothers, and I stayed at the house.

"Sure, I can!"

I jumped at the opportunity to help him.

"Let's just divide everything up by color first. We can start with the whites. Where's the detergent?"

One by one, I pulled each white article of clothing from the basket and tossed it into the washing machine. Nick opened up some cabinets, looking for the detergent.

"Oh, I forgot about this," he said, pointing to his mother's hand-written instructions taped to the inside of the cabinet door.

I peered at the note:

Open lid
Separate clothes by color
Use LIQUID detergent and place in basket
Put clothes in washer
Turn dial to PermaPress cycle
Close lid and press start.

"Nick, is this for real?" I laughed, teetering on genuine inquisition and offending him.

He was quiet. Our eyes locked and my smile faded, realizing I actually had upset him.

"I mean, you guys don't know how to do laundry? Really?"

"No," he said, "Mom does it. Why would we need to know how? Anyway, she put instructions there so we could do it if she wasn't home."

In my home growing up, if I didn't do my own laundry, I went without clean clothes. As a child of a single, working mom, I learned to do things for myself, purely out of necessity. No one babied me the way it seemed Nick and his adult brothers were babied. This was the first time I remember thinking that doing everything for your children was actually a disservice to them.

"Did you guys have chores when you were kids?" I asked.

"Of course we did. I had to clean my bathroom sink and take out the trash."

I was skeptical and somewhat alarmed by the simplicity of the chores and his lack of independence. My judgment must have shown on my face because he quickly began defending his mom and her parenting.

"My mom is a great mom. She was a stay-home mom since she had my oldest brother. She takes care of everything around our house, and we wouldn't be who we are without her. My dad worked a lot and she did everything for us. I love my mom more than anything in this world, so please don't try to insinuate her giving us instructions on laundry is a bad thing."

He handed me the detergent and I poured the blue liquid into the basket, shut the lid, and set the cycle. It was not my intention to upset him. Guilt began to set in. I felt badly, but mostly I was just shocked. No one I knew lived such a pampered life as Nick and his brothers. They didn't want for anything. They had wealthy parents and a stay-home mother who took care of them well into adulthood. Maybe I was jealous. Maybe this wasn't such a bad thing after all. I tried to look at it from his perspective. I tried to be more optimistic and less judgmental.

"I'm sorry. I didn't mean to hurt your feelings," I apologized.

"You just need to know my mom did everything in her power to make sure my brothers and I had a great life. She is an amazing person and I love her. She's a great mom."

"I know. She is amazing and I love her too. She's taken me in and treats me like a daughter. It was wrong of me to judge her."

My offense to his mother wasn't taken well. He was clear I should avoid this type of conflict in the future and to not insinuate negativity or speak ill of her. I waited with nervous anticipation to see if he would forgive me or not. He avoided looking me in the eyes.

"I'm really sorry, Nick. I didn't mean to."

There was a long pause between us, and I waited patiently for him to process his thoughts.

"Don't worry about it," he said, brushing it off and instantly changing his demeanor.

Nick wrapped his arms around me and slid his hands into my jeans pockets, squeezing both of my cheeks tightly.

"You can make it up to me later!"

His attitude went from stern to playful instantly. Mine went from worried to relieved. The rest of our afternoon together would be spent watching television and relaxing around the house. We shared one of the weekly dinners his mom had prepared in the days before they left and then we went for an evening swim in the backyard pool.

As I floated in the warm water next to Nick, I couldn't help but think of how lucky I was to be accepted in his family. Everyone was so normal, and I fit in well. His parents were married still, unlike mine, who were divorced. His siblings were all financially successful, unlike mine who weren't. His family was big and very tight-knit, unlike mine, which was small and separated. I yearned to be part of a perfect family just like this one.

What I didn't know at the time was that Nick's mom, Barbara, had some childhood issues of her own. Those issues would shape her parenting. Issues she desperately tried to keep hidden from the outside world. Things that, in time, would turn unsuspecting children into adult abusers.

CHAPTER 4

DATING – 12 MONTHS

"Do you even love your daughter, Mary?" Nick's eyes were glassy and his voice harsh. There was silence. I was between them on the couch at my mom's house. She stared at him. I could see the anger in her face as she gripped the pillow trying not to rip it in half.

"See, Allie?! She can't even answer me. What kind of parent can't answer a simple question like that about their own child?" His brows furrowed and his eyes shot like lasers at my mother.

I buried my face into my hands, my elbows digging into my thighs. *God please make this stop. Please.*

My tears soaked my palms as I refused to get involved in their argument. I didn't know what to do. My mom stood up from the couch.

"How dare you question my love for my daughter? You are 19 years old. Please, get out of my house. You are not welcome here anymore if you are going to disrespect me that way." The calmness in her voice was almost soothing but cut me deeply.

"No! Mom. Please!" I yelled.

Nick said nothing and stormed out of the house, allowing the screen door to slam behind him. I ran after him and yelled between my sobs for him to wait. My mother had just kicked my boyfriend out of her house. This was my heart ripping in half, and this was exactly what Nick wanted.

"Nick wait!" I yelled.

"I'm never going back to your mom's, Allie. You know she doesn't love you right? You have to know that."

There was immense pressure in my eyes and my nose was stuffed from crying. I sniffled and wiped my face with my shirt's sleeve as I waited for him to unlock the car. We jumped into his black sedan and sped off to his mom and dad's house.

"My mom does love me," I whimpered, unsure if I was trying to convince myself or convince Nick.

"Are you serious? She couldn't even answer me when I asked her. She doesn't love you. She only wants you to pay her rent because she has no money. She's a bad mom, Allie. My mom would never ask my brothers or me to pay rent. You need to realize she is a bad mom and she doesn't love you. I'm sorry. I know it must be really difficult to hear, but it's true and you know I would never lie to you." He reached over and wiped a tear from my cheek.

I didn't want to believe him. I didn't want him to be right. I knew my mother needed money. If I was going to live there while in college, she said I had to pay. I was angry. I felt slighted. I had the money to help out, but I didn't want to.

"I guess you're right," I said between sobs. "I'll call my dad and see if I can stay there."

My dad lived an hour away, but Nick was fully on board with this decision. It would be more difficult for us to see each other but not only was he supportive, he encouraged it. He felt it would be better for me if I were away from my mom, even if it meant being away from him too.

Barbara was hanging up the phone as Nick and I walked in and plopped down at the kitchen table.

"Well, that was an interesting phone call," she said.

"Who was it?" asked Nick.

"Your mother."

A flash of panic rushed over me and I perked up.

"My mother? What did she say?"

"Well, she told me that you were very rude to her." Barbara glared at her son, waiting for him to tell her it wasn't true.

"I wasn't rude to her! She wouldn't even say she loves Allie! What kind of mom does that? Look at her. Look how sad she is! She can't stop crying. All Mary cares about is money. Allie works and has good grades and she still expects her to pay rent. That's just stupid."

My broken heart was starting to feel better as my boyfriend defended me at the expense of my mom. Barbara walked over to me, put her arm around my shoulder and squeezed me with a loving touch. My eyes still hurt from crying and no air was getting through my nasal passages.

"Oh sweetie. Don't worry. Everything will be just fine. No matter what, we all love you. We all care about you here. We know you are a good girl doing your best. I don't think it's right to make my kids pay rent when they're doing their best to work and keep up good grades. It just isn't right. If you were my daughter, I certainly wouldn't do that to you."

The phone rang. I nodded as I absorbed her words and settled in on my confusion.

"Hello," Barb said.

The voice coming through the speaker was so loud both Nick and I could hear.

"Where are my paper plates?"

"What are you talking about Mother?"

"You know what I'm talking about Barb. You threw them away, didn't you?!" the gruff voice barked through the speaker.

"Are you talking about your *used* paper plates? Yes, I threw those away because you can't be using dirty paper plates more than one time. It's not sanitary."

"You have no right to come over here and do that behind my back! Do you think you can just do whatever you want? This is my house!"

Nick and I remained quiet to eavesdrop as his mom and grandmother continued to argue. Nicks grandmother was quite the spitfire. She was always sweet to me but had a hard time remembering my name, constantly calling me Abby. She was overly loud, aggressive, and quite demanding of Barbara. Barbara made sure she met all of her mother's needs, but it seemed she could never live up to Grandmother's expectations. She criticized Barbara regularly. Like clockwork, her daughter tried to please her, rarely meeting those expectations.

"Goodbye, Mother."

Barbara hung up and sat down at the table with us. We discussed what happened at my mom's and I poured my heart out to my boyfriend's mother. I reveled in the calmness and love I felt from her. *Why couldn't my mom be like her?*

Several days later, I began packing all of my things from my mom's house and started to move in with my dad and stepmom. They were eager to have me, and I wasn't required to pay them. I don't remember speaking to my mom much that day. I was bitter and anxious to leave. I began to believe she didn't love me, and, over time, Nick would drive home more and more reasons why.

The distance between my mother and me widened over the years, and though she always reached out, I was quick to end conversations and made lots of excuses as to why we couldn't come around. She forgave Nick, even though he never apologized, and she eventually allowed him back into her house. I think she realized I would never come unless he was with me, and she was right.

I was enveloped in my new family. His mother and his siblings replaced mine. My dad was the only one who never got replaced. Nick knew he couldn't take everyone away from me, and my dad was one of the few people he thought he could manipulate easily. I was scared to lose my father since I had already lost most of my family to Nick's isolation. I hid the bad parts of our relationship from my dad and acted like life was great. I kept the truth hidden for years, and it is still one of the biggest regrets of my life.

Though I couldn't see it at the time, Nick began to see my mother as a threat very early in our relationship. She stood up to him and set clear boundaries with how he could treat her. Of course, Nick didn't like boundaries and he wasn't accustomed to anyone challenging him. He knew she would be hard to erase from my life, but he tried his best over the years to do so anyway.

She hung on like any loving mother would. She kept clawing her way back after I pushed her away or shut her out. She never gave up. She never knew the extent of what I was enduring with Nick because I wasn't even aware of it. What she did know was her beloved daughter was slipping away.

Eventually, I came to terms with the fact my boyfriend and mother were never going to get along. I reluctantly accepted that it would be a tumultuous road for me as long as Nick and I were together. This conflict drove me straight into the arms of *the best mom in the world*, Barbara.

CHAPTER 5

ENGAGED – 18 MONTHS INTO RELATIONSHIP

"I'd like to pay for your wedding dress," my mom whispered in my ear as she hugged me, "I'm really happy for you."

Her voice quivered and she hugged me tighter. I caught my joyful expression in the mirror behind her just outside the fitting room.

"Wow, Mom. Thank you so much! You don't have to do that!"

She held my shoulders, pulled back to get a look at me. Her eyes were glassy as she looked me over.

"You look absolutely gorgeous in this dress."

"Thanks Mom."

"How much is the dress anyway?" Barbara butted in, fumbling around all the silky folds of fabric to find the price tag.

"Here it is," she said, "Wow, this thing's $600.00. Are you sure about this one? I thought you and Nick talked about $400.00."

"I love this dress. It's my wedding. I don't care that it's $600.00."

"It's your AND Nick's wedding, dear."

"Well, my mom said she wants to buy it anyway, so it won't come out of our budget."

"What is Nick going to think about you going over budget?"

My mom shot me a glance of disapproval. There was quite the contention between my mother and Barbara. They both seemed to be fighting for first place. Though no one could truly take the place of my mom, Barbara seemed determined to make that change.

Barbara helped me out of the dress in the fitting room.

"You know, I brought something with me for you to try on."

"You did?"

Barbara reached into her large handbag and unwrapped a long sheer wedding veil.

"It's what I wore on my wedding day. My mother made it."

Without waiting for my objection, she placed a crown of fabric flowers on my head. They were aged in yellow and appeared as if they had been soaked in nicotine. The sheer trail of off-white material draped along my back clashed with the stark white sheen of my dress. My intention was not to offend my mother-in-law to-be, so I smiled at myself in the mirror and lied to her telling her how pretty her veil was.

"You can wear it for your wedding if you want to. We can clean it up so it matches."

"Wow, that's really nice of you. I might want to have one made. Maybe you can help?"

"Oh, of course! I'd be happy to."

After I put on my clothes, we walked to the register to meet my mom and bridesmaids. Barbara pulled me to the side and told me she wanted to pay for the dress using her credit card because she would be able to get extra Sky miles from points on her card. I explained to her a second time that my mom wanted to pay for my dress, but Barbara kept pushing me about using her card.

"Your mom can just give you the cash and then you can give it to me," she explained.

My mom was upset and offended as I explained the situation to her under the pressure of my soon-to-be mother-in-law. I felt stuck in the middle of an argument I didn't need or want to be involved in.

Barbara was becoming extra insistent about using her credit card and called Nick to reinforce her stance. My mom's eyes were glassy. She held her head high, but it was evident she was holding back tears. There was an invisible tug of war happening between them and I was the rope.

After discreetly giving Nick the details, Barbara held the phone out in front of my face. I quickly snatched it from her hand and put it to my ear. Each of my bridesmaids and my mother were standing by, waiting to see what I would say. Even I didn't know what I would say to Nick. Wedding dress shopping was supposed to be fun. Nothing about this experience was fun. It was completely stressful and unenjoyable.

"Hey." I said.

"Why am I being bothered with this stupid dress issue right now at work?"

"Your mom is the one who called, not me!"

Barbara shrugged her shoulders at me as I locked eyes with her.

"I don't care who called. I want to know why you all can't figure this out on your own? I actually have a job to do if you didn't notice."

"I just don't know what to do because your mom is wanting to pay for the dress, but my mom offered first, and I don't want to hurt either of their feelings."

My mother and mother-in-law to-be stood on either side of me. The tension surrounded us like a thick cloud of smoke. Formica was chipping away on the checkout counter and I dug my fingernail underneath, mindlessly picking at it as I listened to Nick complain. The customer service lady behind the counter nonchalantly slid her business card across the counter over the chip and forced my hand away to keep me from doing more damage. Embarrassed, I quickly pulled my hand back and mouthed to her, "I'm sorry." Everyone was waiting on me, but Nick kept on lecturing.

"Just have Mom pay for it. You and your mom are just making this more complicated than it needs to be."

I didn't want to argue, especially not here, not now, and not in front of everyone. Having his mom pay for the dress was not what I wanted. This would create a bigger divide between my mom and me. I hated the thought of deliberately hurting anyone.

Barbara took the phone back from me and put it in her purse. I could see her getting out her credit card in my peripheral vision. I stared directly at the lady behind the counter but felt the heat of my mother and Barbara staring at me.

"Will this be cash or credit today ma'am?"

Sasha worked her way in between Barbara and me and put her hand on my shoulder. I reached inside my purse, opened my wallet and handed the lady my own credit card. Barbara couldn't help herself and spoke up.

"Allie!"

"Credit card. I'll be using MY credit card," I said firmly and directly to the cashier.

My mother was silent and stone faced. Barbara's eyes squinted toward me and her hands clutched tightly onto her purse strap. The clerk swiped my card and handed it back to me. Sasha kept her hand steady on my shoulder until after the transaction was complete. Nick would find out I didn't let his mom pay. But he'd also know I didn't let my mom pay either. It was the only real solution I could see at the time. The argument and lecture I'd get later would be easier to endure than letting down my mom.

Everything played out as I predicted when I got home. Nick and I got into an argument because I had made my own decision and didn't follow his rules. The next morning as I was leaving for work, I discovered a letter he wrote me to express his disappointment. It was folded up in an envelope placed under the windshield wiper of my car. I tore it open, unfolded the paper, and stood there in the driveway, absorbing the words on the page.

Allie,

I am kind of disappointed in you. You put in the budget, a dress of $450, tops. You said you could get it cheaper. I have a feeling even though you said you wouldn't let that happen, that Sasha's influence on you has led you to want to buy a more expensive dress. In a perfect world, you could buy a $5,000 dress but you have to realize we are under a budget here. Mom and I are trying so hard to save everywhere we can, and you seem like you will spend however much you want. If your mom helps pay, that is one thing, but we are already over budget by $500 to $1,000, not to mention another $200 to $300 for the dress. Planning weddings are a good indication for how a marriage will be, and right now I don't feel like you're a partner and that hurts. I really try to listen to you and heed *your advice. Do you do the same? I love you so much and I want to kill any problems before they start. If I'm going to buy us a nice house, we need all the money we can get, remember that.*

> *I love you,*
> *Nick*

The argument was finished that night, but Nick couldn't let it go. I was angry. I crumpled the paper in my hands and marched back into the house to call him. My solution was the best solution. He needed to hear my reasoning again. As I flung open the door and went for the phone, it rang. I recognized the number right away. Mom.

Ugh. What does she want? Should I answer? I don't have time for this.

The phone rang again. I reached for it and fixated on the caller ID.

Dammit. I answered and put the phone to my ear.

"Hello?"

"Hi, it's Mom."

"I know. I saw it on caller ID." Irritation bubbled over in my voice.

"Are you okay? You sound funny."

"Funny?" I asked, clearly annoyed.

"Oh I don't know. I'm sorry. Are you busy?" she stammered.

"Not really. What's up?" *Get to the point, Mom. What do you want?*

"I don't mean to bother you, but I was wondering if we could get together this weekend and go see a movie?" Her voice rose to a higher pitch. She was hopeful.

"Um. Well, we have plans this weekend," I lied.

Nick's guttural voice replayed in my head, rehearsed and ready for situations like these.

"Make something up Allie. I don't care what you have to say. You have better things to do than hang out with your mom."

"Oh, you have plans *all* weekend?" She was suspicious, but she certainly wasn't stupid.

"I mean, not *all* weekend, but we are busy, and I don't know how we will find time. We have plans with some friends of ours and some stuff going on with Nick's family. I just don't know how we can make it work."

I wondered if she could tell that I was lying. Mothers can always tell when their children are lying. I cringed waiting for her response. There was a long pause.

"Oh," she said sadly. "Well, maybe the following weekend?" Her voice cracked a little as she tried to hold back her emotions.

"I don't know, Mom, I'll need to look at my calendar and talk to Nick. We'll just have to see. I'm just really busy all the time with wedding planning and stuff. It's really tough, you know?" I spit the rancid lies from my mouth. My mother's voice quivered.

"I just really miss you. That's all."

I swallowed the guilt whole. It sat in my gut like a cold stone. But the stone-cold guilt was way easier to swallow than what Nick would be shoving down my throat if I didn't follow his orders. I always weighed out the consequences, and almost every time, Nick's were heavier. I didn't know what to say.

"I'll figure something out and I'll let you know."

I was torn between hurting my mother and protecting myself. I chose the latter every opportunity I had. My mother would always love me, no matter how badly I hurt her. I despised myself for abusing that. I tried to push it out of my mind, regardless of how tenaciously it clawed the surface of my mind. Love from Nick was not unconditional, so I had to do what would make him happy to avoid being crushed under the weight of his unhappiness with me.

The aching in my heart was still lingering, though. I was a terrible daughter. I felt like I had no choice. I was weak. I plunged a sharp knife of regret deep inside my mother's heart so Nick couldn't stab me with it. Inevitably, naivety clouded my head. Nick had an arsenal of other weapons to use against me and I was willing to do anything to eliminate just one, even at the expense of my own mother.

In Nick's letter to me, his statement said, *planning weddings are a good indication of how a marriage will be.* Upon reading this, I should have run far away from him. But I didn't, because his words made me doubt myself. He made me think he was right and I was wrong. But, if I had actually considered the condescension, the manipulation and the control in this letter, I could have easily predicted how the marriage would transpire. As it turned out, it was all those things I didn't see.

Nick was effectively able to turn the entire scenario into my fault. He was easily able to toy with my emotions and create doubt in my mind about my ability to make my own decisions. In just a few sentences, he was able to make me second-guess my ability to recall details of the situation without him ever being there. He could solicit apologies from me with ease for the error of my ways. This was the beginning of the end. If I could have read between the lines, I could have seen the deception at play. This kind of behavior is very difficult to recognize as bad or wrong, especially for someone who's never experienced it.

CHAPTER 6

WEDDING DAY – 2 YEARS INTO RELATIONSHIP

I can do this. I told myself as I sat waiting in the Priest's changing room with my dad. The church was packed full of our family and friends. Hummingbirds buzzed in the pit of my stomach. *These don't feel like butterflies.* My dad brushed the delicate veil off my bare shoulder and rested his strong hand on my back.

"Are you doing alright?" he asked, sensing my emotional unrest. I breathed out slowly holding both hands onto my abdomen.

"I don't know, Dad. Does everyone get cold feet before they get married? I'm not sure I can do this. I feel a little sick."

I mowed right over the multitude of red flags lining my path to this church. I wasn't in love with Nick. I was in love with the future that Nick sold to me. I looked at him with hopes of what he could become when I should have looked at him for what he really was. My reality and my fantasy for Nick's potential weren't even on the same planet.

My sparkly diamond sat perched on four prongs supported by a shiny, gold band and I stared at it as I tried to quell my feelings of disappointment. *Be grateful, it's a pretty diamond.* I didn't like the gold. Nick knew I never wore gold jewelry, but he insisted I would eventually. He claimed it looked better on me. The diamond caught the sunlight as I maneuvered my hand from side to side. Nick insisted that I would get tired of silver jewelry and I'd be happy to have a yellow gold ring someday. *Maybe I would get used to a gold ring?*

"Aw, honey, you'll be alright," he assured me. His kind eyes filled with concern as he blinked behind his round glasses.

"I think everyone has some nerves before they get married. Once you see him, I'm sure you'll feel better. I love you, sweetheart. You are so beautiful. Just look at you. I never could have imagined you'd be this stunning at 21 looking back to when you were just a little girl. I always told you to stay little but you didn't listen to me!" He laughed.

"Well, I kind of listened, I'm still only five feet tall!"

He held out his hand for me, and as I took it, he helped me out of the chair. My balance was off as I rose, and I almost fell backwards.

"Woah there!" he chuckled, as he steadied me. I obtained my balance on my wedding heels and he pulled me upright.

"I'd really prefer not to carry you down the aisle today, but I will if I have to. No broken bones 'til after I walk you down okay?"

I laughed and threw my arms around his neck. The scruff of his beard lightly scratched my cheek.

"I love you, Dad."

"I love you, too, sweetheart."

I took his muscular arm with my right hand and squeezed the slick stems of my rose bouquet with my left. A big burst of air expelled from my lungs. *You love Nick so much. This is the happiest day of your life. This is a happy day. Don't be scared.*

The church doors opened wide and the sweet guitar strings of "Pachelbel's Canon in D" lured us down the aisle. Everyone stood and turned to look at me. My mother and Nick's parents were smiling at the front of the church. Friends and family members were taking pictures as my father guided me slowly towards my groom. As I got nearer, I noticed Nick's lower lip quivering. His hands were folded in front of him. He looked more nervous than me. This was it. There was no turning back now. We were getting married.

"A reading from Corinthians 13: 4 – 8. Love is patient, love is kind. It does not envy, it does not boast, it is not proud. It does not dishonor others, it is not self-seeking, it is not easily angered, it keeps no record of wrongs. Love does not delight in evil but rejoices with the truth. It always protects, always trusts, always hopes, always perseveres."

My older brother finished the reading and quietly exited the podium. Beside Nick were his two older brothers as The Best Man and Groomsmen. My brother's place would not be allowed in the wedding party, but Nick did permit him to do a reading in our wedding. At my side were two of my three closest friends. Nick did not approve of the fourth so she passed out programs at the front of the church.

Up until the very second I said 'I do,' I constantly permitted Nick's bad behavior. He controlled every aspect of our relationship; he controlled every aspect of our engagement and he controlled almost every aspect of our wedding day. He would also control every aspect of the rest of our lives together.

"I now pronounce you, Nicholas and Allison Adrian!" the priest announced.

The entire congregation stood and applauded. Cameras flashed from the pews like nighttime fireflies. I caught a glimpse of my mother wiping her eye with a tissue. *Those aren't happy tears.* My brother put his arm around her shoulder, and she forced a smile.

Nick and I held hands and he helped me down the steps. I was relieved it was over. He squeezed my hand, and I felt his gold band on his ring finger. I looked up at him, and he raised his eyebrows at me and bent over to whisper in my ear.

"Hello wife."

"We're married!" I exclaimed.

Nick smiled, I smiled and everyone else smiled with us. The sun was blasting in from the stained-glass windows. Everyone stood and clapped as we happily walked down the aisle.

The air conditioning in the undercroft was cold and refreshing from the stuffy church. I stared at Nick as he joked and chatted with his brothers and my friends. We'd made a vow in front of our friends and family and God to love and honor and cherish each other. But it was a sly trick he did to me. It was an unreachable goal. It was a myth, a fairy tale, and a supernatural dream. None of it was real. Our vows were important to me and I intended to keep them. Little did I know that Nick didn't intend to keep them at all. I was too naïve to know that when you fall in love with someone's potential, you are setting yourself up for failure. All of my hope was clinging to *what could be* when in reality it *never would have been.*

The wedding party followed behind us and we all shuffled around the wedding tables. A hint of sweet champagne tickled my nostrils as Sasha shoved a glass up under my nose.

"Here, I'll take that." Nick said, taking a swig of the champagne.

"Hey," Sasha yelled, "that was for Allie."

"We have like ten bottles; I'm getting my drink on! Pour her another!"

He planted a big champagne kiss right on my lips. Sasha just looked at me with a straight face. She wasn't amused.

Once all of the guests settled into the reception area, we went through the scheduled events of cake cutting, tossing the bouquet, and first dances. We were making rounds to say hello to family and friends when Nick was pulled away by one of his high school buddies.

"It's okay," I agreed. "Go on and talk to your friends."

I continued alone thanking the guests and talking with as many people as I could. Time had passed quickly and before I knew it, there wasn't much time left in the night. I hadn't seen Nick since he'd gone with his friend and I began to look for him.

"Have you seen Nick anywhere?" I asked Barbara.

"No honey, I haven't, is everything okay?" she asked.

"Oh, yeah, I just haven't seen him in a while."

I walked all around the reception hall, flashing smiles and sneaking hugs in until I finally found Nick sitting at a round table with a big group of his friends. They were playing "quarters," and Nick had his tie around his head like Rambo. When his friends saw me, they all cheered loudly.

"Hey! Hey!" they yelled, laughing and smiling, slapping Nick on the back and spilling their beers. Nick had a dopey look on his face and his eyes were heavy. It wasn't worth a fight on our wedding day. I smiled and greeted his friends and then found guests on the dance floor. I spent the rest of the reception dancing, while my new husband played bar games at a table at the back of the hall.

CHAPTER 7

MARRIED – 1 YEAR

Dog piss soaked the concrete floor of the kennel where the gray, wire-haired puppy was sitting. His eyes focused on me as I approached the metal fencing between us. His tail flitted back and forth, and he scooted on his rear closer to me to stick his shiny, wet nose through the gaps in the chain links. I reached out my hand and his warm, pink tongue gently licked my fingers. His hair was matted. He'd clearly been neglected for some time. The info tag on the cage read, "Blackie." I giggled. He wasn't even black. He was going to need a new name.

"Hey buddy," I sang in a high-pitched tone, trying to reach in to pet him. He pressed his wet muzzle through as far as it would go. I got a closer look at him. He had the prettiest brown eyes framed in eyelashes at least an inch long. Something about him was very special. I knew I had to have him.

"Nick! Come here! You have to look at this dog. He's the ugliest little thing I've ever seen," I laughed, "but isn't he adorable!?"

Nick cringed and placed his face in the crook of his inner elbow.

"He smells awful."

"I don't care. I want him. I can clean him up. I'll give him a bath and a haircut. If we don't adopt him, nobody else will take him, and they will euthanize him. Look how sweet he is." I begged for Nick to say yes.

Blackie's little ears perked up. He was on his best behavior. He never whined or barked once. It seemed he knew had to be polite, if he was going to get a forever home. He sat patiently and waited as Nick and I talked about which dog to take home.

"Oh, wow, are you sure?" Nick asked skeptically.

"Yes, he's the one! If we don't adopt this one, they will euthanize him. Please. We need to rescue him. He's the one!" I shrieked.

It didn't take much pleading for Nick to say yes. He had wanted a dog too. We were newly married and we both wanted a pet. Nick bent down and petted the little dog through the cage. He wagged his tail and licked Nick's hand.

"Hey bud, are you a good boy?" Nick said, talking sweetly to the pup.

"See, he's really sweet, isn't he?!"

Nick stood up.

"Yeah, he seems like he might be a pretty good dog."

Blackie tilted his head to the side as if he were trying to understand our conversation. I could see the yearning in his eyes. He was meant to be mine. Nick left the decision up to me.

"If you want him and you can train him, then I'm good with him."

"Yes!" I squealed.

We went through all of the paperwork, signed the documents, and paid the small adoption fee to bring our new dog home. There was something about this dog that I couldn't pinpoint, but I just knew he was going to be an exceptional pet. There was something in the way he looked at me. He looked miserable in the cage, but he still had hope and love in his eyes. Maybe, looking back, I subconsciously saw myself in that poor little pup and I needed to rescue him.

We took him home and I gave him a warm, comfortable bath, three separate times in the stationary tub of our basement. I could tell he didn't love the bath, but he tolerated it. He shivered and quaked, not from cold, but from anxiety I suppose. He gave my hands soft licks as I massaged the baby shampoo into his fur. He calmed down and seemed to enjoy the loving touch he'd been yearning for. He was a pathetic little thing, but I would soon find out he would be one of the smartest, most obedient and loving animals I would ever come to love.

My affection for him grew and grew. Though he wasn't perfect at first, I was easily able to train him to have excellent manners. His sweet demeanor was already in his DNA. He was an extremely submissive dog and aimed to please. Being a fast learner, I was able to teach him lots of tricks in the first year we had him. I spent hours each day rewarding him with treats and praise when he succeeded.

He was a joy to be with. He was an amazing dog worthy of all the love and attention in the world. So that's what I named him: Worthy.

CHAPTER 8

Married – 2 Years

The haunting sound of the enormous organ pipes behind us flooded the church. I rested my weight into the thin pleather of the kneeler beneath me as I tried to concentrate and pray. The pain stung my knees while gravity pulled at me. The padding was worn. I couldn't hold my position anymore from the pain, so I slid my butt slowly into the pew while my forehead rested on my folded hands. Abruptly, I felt Nick's elbow stab into my rib cage. *Jerk.*

"What?" I whispered.

He motioned to me to get back into my kneeling position.

"My knees are hurting." I grumbled.

His eyes glared at me with hatred and disapproval.

"If Jesus handled that pain," he whispered, nodding at the carved crucifix hanging above the alter, "then you can handle being on your knees for a few minutes."

I carefully placed my knees back into the shallow dents of the kneeler and tried to concentrate on Jesus. *I hate you, Nick.* I tried to push the anger out of my heart while I was in God's house. I prayed Jesus would take the hate from my heart, but all I wanted to do was run.

This was Nick's church from birth, not mine. I was here because of Nick. Every week, without fail, Nick was in church. It didn't matter if Nick was on vacation or out of town for work. He did not miss Catholic Mass, ever.

Initially, I admired him and his dedication. I went to church with him weekly. I asked a lot of questions of him and afterwards of the priest. *"Why do they do this?" "Why do they say that?" "Why aren't there Bibles in the pews?"* Finally, after much frustration at my childlike inquisition, the priest suggested I take RCIA (The Rights of Christian Initiation of Adults) classes and learn about the Catholic faith. I was open to learning and I yearned to know more, so I agreed.

I began to love the Catholic religion. Fully immersing myself into it filled me with love and hope. It would be where I would turn to in some of the darkest times of my life. It was a beautiful and serene place, but I soon learned it was also the place where Nick liked to hide. Every weekend, he put on his Sunday best and slipped into a cloak of camouflage to conceal his true identity.

He convinced the world he was a good person. The entire community would view this positively as well. There might be a possibility he benefited from attending church, but he used it, and God, to hide his evil ways. As he sat solemnly, eyes gazed at the crucifix, he was theoretically hiding behind the cross. It was a complete hypocrisy and it completely fooled me.

When I met Nick, I knew he was a Catholic. I knew he attended mass regularly, even during college, but I didn't know he sat in the pew each week because it helped him to hide the demons living inside him. *"What a great guy!"* I used to think. *"He's smart, he's funny, and he's a good Christian who attends church like clockwork. He's devoted and dedicated. He's a good person."* Oh, how I was so very wrong.

After the evening mass was over, we stayed to chat with relatives and friends as the rest of the parishioners dispersed like slow cattle. There was a lot of small talk and smiles and I stayed in Nick's shadow until we got back to our car where the mood immediately shifted. Nick did not like my actions in church and his haughty demeanor was my punishment. It didn't bother me too much. It was either a lecture or the silent treatment, and I preferred the latter.

Stomach acid churned inside me as a small disk of unleavened bread and church wine sat mingling in my gut. The gurgling was soft yet audible in the midst of his stonewalling. I regretted skipping lunch. *I'm so hungry.* I pushed my clenched fists into my belly and leaned forward into my seatbelt. Nick didn't seem to notice. The car idled.

A light tapping on my window snatched my attention. Nick's mom Barbara was standing outside my door smiling. He lowered my window from the driver's side controls.

"What are you doing leaned over like that, girl?" she laughed.

"Oh, I'm starving, that's all." I shot her a big smile.

"Well, let's go get something for supper then. Do you guys want to go with us?"

Nick's dad was waiting impatiently in his shiny, clean sedan. I looked up and waved at him, but he pretended he didn't see me. I looked at Nick to gauge his interest in dinner with his mom and dad. He shrugged his shoulders indifferently.

"Sure. Fine." he said.

"What is wrong with *you*?" His mother asked him.

"Would you please tell her Catholics are supposed to kneel when the congregation kneels?" he blurted.

"Well I think she knows that. Why do I need to tell her?"

Barbara fanned herself with the church bulletin and the loose curls around her face lifted.

"Hot flash," she sighed.

"Never mind, Mom."

"My knees were hurting, so I sat up," I said, defending my decision.

Barbara couldn't resist the urge to get involved, and we both were hoping she'd take each of our sides. Nick's dad, Mike, tapped his horn twice.

"Oh, would you just wait a second!" she snapped at him across the lot.

She turned back to us and poked her head into my window with a smile. Cherry Blossom lotion mixed with spearmint gum wafted in.

"Everyone in church can see you're not kneeling, but most importantly, Jesus can. It's just best to deal with hurt knees."

Barbara wasn't suggesting this to me. She was telling me. Her words were soft and motherly. This wasn't what I wanted to hear, but I knew she would give her opinion about it whether or not she was asked. She changed the subject abruptly after my silence.

"You aren't going to believe what your sister-in-law did yesterday."

"Who? Amy?" Nick asked.

"Your brother was telling me. You can't say anything because I'm not supposed to repeat it, but he caught her sneaking food out of the pantry last night."

Barbara's eyes widened. She waited for one of us to chastise my sister-in-law behind her back. She eagerly anticipated us joining in on her gossip.

"Sneaking food? How do you sneak food in your own house?" I asked, full well knowing you don't, and Nick's brother, Bart, was a complete control freak.

"She's on a diet," Barbara said, attempting to justify Bart's behavior.

My sister-in-law, Amy, wasn't overweight. She struggled with a few extra pounds, but Bart was extremely critical of her body. He monitored her portion sizes, made recommendations of what her choices should be, and expressed disapproval if she reached for anything unhealthy. I watched this happen frequently and I spoke up many times to defend her.

Amy and I were friends, and we often exercised together. We ran a 5K race once, and it was a huge accomplishment for her after training for months in preparation. She worked hard to keep herself healthy, but I watched as her husband melted away her self-worth like a hot knife in butter.

"All right, Mom, let's just go. Dad's getting annoyed," he barked.

Nick's impatience was emerging. He was close with his mom, but he never hesitated to put her in her place and she always permitted it.

I was looking forward to dinner and gossiping with my in-laws. Shining the spotlight on someone else was my way of keeping it off of me. I would try to play intermediary and still defend Amy against her husband. But, secretly, I enjoyed conversing about other people's private affairs. I only felt a slight amount of guilt. I knew my mother-in-law went from sibling to sibling churning up the scum that belonged to other people, even Nick's and mine. I just didn't care. We were bonding and sharing secrets within the family bubble. It was a simple way for me to feel better about my own failing relationship.

"Come…on…Barb!" Mike droned as each word slowly emphasized his frustration.

She rolled her eyes at us and shook her head.

"I'm coming, you old butthead!" she shouted back.

"He is so impatient sometimes."

Nick and I drove to meet them at the restaurant where we stuffed our bellies with food and each other's minds with negativity. The conversations were almost always about someone else's faults in the eyes of Barbara Adrian. And no matter what the church homily was that week, no matter what the bible readings were, it was never enough to snuff out the hypocrisy of it all. Repeatedly, I permitted myself to be an integral part of it every single time.

Initially, upon meeting them, I thought Nick and his family were good Christian people. They appeared to be godly and dedicated to their faith. His siblings, aunts, uncles, cousins and grandparents all were a big part of the community church to which they belonged. In the presence of the public eye, they seemed to be a well-oiled machine, treating each other with kindness and respect. I would soon learn it's what you do behind closed doors, outside of the church and in between Sundays, that actually matters the most.

CHAPTER 9

MARRIED – 3 YEARS

The first time I had to give myself a Clomid shot, I was already leaning towards adoption. After several years of trying, I just couldn't get pregnant and I was frustrated with the process. Fertility doctors, prescription pills, monthly shots, and lots of cold, loveless sex was the recipe for conceiving a biological child. My reproductive system refused to cooperate, and it was beginning to take a heavy toll.

Trying to conceive the traditional way turned sex into a chore, and we hadn't been preventing pregnancy for a few years. There was nothing fun or enjoyable about it. It just wasn't sexy. It was simply an act of conception, sterile-like and lacking emotion. But this wasn't unusual of our marital sex life, and I didn't really know any differently.

On Nick's end, there was no talking, no moaning, not even heavy breathing. There were no sounds, no loving words, no smiles, no nothing. Our sex life lacked passion.

Ultimately, I thought he was just focusing on the act itself, but I often felt like I was having sex with a prop or a blow-up doll. There was no intimacy, and there was a complete lack of feeling of closeness between us. Eye contact was rare, and Nick always wanted the lights out.

Being a mother was always a dream of mine. Nick wanted a big family, and after being married for a few years, we decided it was time to grow our own. We tried to conceive without medical intervention for two years, which included checking my basal temperature, my cervical mucous (yes, that's a thing), and sticking my legs up in the air after sex. After those efforts didn't result in the little baby we'd been wishing for, we turned to a reproductive specialist. Next steps were medicines I couldn't pronounce, shots in the thighs, and artificial insemination where his sperm got turkey basted into my uterus.

Nick's sperm count was high, but my body wasn't ready for a baby. Our intercourse conception efforts would be replaced by my husband jerking off into a plastic cup I kept warm between my thighs on a mad dash to the fertility office. His little glob of sperm would be placed delicately and inserted timely into my womb as we prayed God would let one stick.

Time and again, I lay there with my legs propped in stirrups on the sterile exam table staring at the fluorescent light above me. We would have to wait two, excruciatingly long weeks and pray my period wouldn't arrive.

Eventually, after attempting this method five times, I was finally pregnant! Nine months later, our prayers were answered, and our healthy, tiny, beautiful Claire was born. After we brought our new daughter home from the hospital,

I informed my employer I wouldn't be returning to my corporate job, which I'd held successfully since we'd been married. Both of my parents were part of the blue-collar working class, so being a stay at home mom wasn't something I was familiar with. Nick suggested I stay home from work because his job could afford us the luxury of me being a full-time mom. It was a sad but exciting time for me. I would be able to stay home with my beloved daughter and see all of her firsts and raise her myself. I knew I would miss my co-workers and the sense of accomplishment one gets from hard work and earning a paycheck. What I never anticipated missing was my independence.

I was no longer contributing to the bank account. I was no longer making my own decisions regarding our finances. Suddenly, I felt as if I were spending Nick's money, not our money. My purchases required his permission, and he analyzed my receipts to ensure I wasn't overspending. My questions about money were dismissed because he said I wouldn't understand. I didn't feel like his partner. I felt like his child. It was evident he didn't trust me to responsibly spend, and he didn't think I was intelligent enough to understand the complexities of investing. Over time, I began to believe these lies, which resulted in Nick gaining more power over me.

"After all," he'd say, *"we don't have as much money as we used to without your income, and we are supporting another person now."* He had a point. The math wasn't wrong. My salary was half of his and then it was gone. We had one more mouth to feed and quite a significant amount of money from my salary would no longer be coming in.

So, I tried my best to be careful about my spending. As Nick instructed, I checked the price per ounce on all my grocery purchases. I used coupons whenever I could, and I tried to only buy the less expensive store brand items to save extra money. Combining trips would save on gas, so I did my best to plan out trips in advance. Inevitably, Nick still complained I'd spent too much or too carelessly.

"We don't need this. Why did you buy this? Don't buy this kind of thing again. Save the receipts for everything in case you need to take something back."

After a purchase, Nick would inspect what I bought to determine if he thought it was valid. He rummaged through my bags scrutinizing items and their corresponding prices. If you've ever approached the exit of a department store with your bags, and the alarm goes off, then you know how this feels. An associate comes over and looks through your bags and you immediately get anxious. You didn't steal anything. You paid for all of your merchandise fairly. But you know you're being watched. You know customers and salesclerks are staring at you, wondering what you stole.

My own partner had no trust in my ability to spend money. It was hurtful, frustrating, and insulting. *What did I do to deserve this mistrust? Why does he think I'm irresponsible? Is it true I may have bought things he wouldn't buy? Yes.* But never had I been irresponsible with money, and I'd never come close to putting our family in financial peril.

With Nick at the head of the theoretical boardroom table, my purchasing power could be revoked. My credit card could be taken without notice. I feared buying things. He was withholding power from me to make informed purchases without his permission. The immense pressure to obey his financial orders kept me in a position of submission. He made the money. He earned the paycheck. The microscope on my credit cards and receipts were enough to start a vicious cycle of anxiety that would be deeply ingrained in me for years.

After Claire was born, then came our daughter, Lleyton, and soon after that came our little boy, Carter. Three beautiful children completed our family, and I felt so blessed to have them all. But with each child born, a little more of me died. Not because of my children, because of Nick. My independence was stripped, and he held a magnifying glass on my every move. My parenting was criticized. My choices were questioned. Money wasn't the only thing under tight control. Everything was. If Nick didn't agree, it was wrong and there was no convincing him otherwise.

Losing my independence almost seemed like a payment for getting the reward of being a stay-home mom. Never did Nick tell me I'd lose my autonomy. Never did he say that being a mom would slowly erase my equality with him. Never did Nick even allude to the fact that quitting my career would set him in a position of power over me I couldn't fathom. Being able to raise my children was a gift many people are not afforded. I felt lucky and privileged. But what I didn't know was that Nick was stealthily making me his prisoner. It was like a frog in a pot of water. You turn up the heat gradually and ever so slowly, and the frog never notices the water beginning to boil. Eventually, the frog just dies.

Raising my three kids full time was rewarding. There is no doubt about it. But if turning back the clock were an option, I would have held onto my professional independence for as long as possible, even if it meant working part-time.

My husband knew exactly what he was doing when he dangled the "stay-home mom" carrot in front of me. He wanted his family to be a clone of the one his parents made. He wanted me to be just like his mother. Because of the luxury I was afforded to stay home with my daughter, it seemed like there wasn't a choice. We could afford it, so I should stay home.

The pressure was amplified from Nick's parents. Barbara and I discussed my sister-in-law considering staying home and she wasn't shy about her opinions. *"What kind of mother wouldn't want to be at home with their child? Why on earth would you choose to let someone else raise your child if you can afford to do it yourself? How selfish must you be?"* She even refused to watch any of her grandkids without payment. *If you're going to go back to work and pay a daycare, then you can pay me too.* They didn't need the money. She just didn't want her son's wives going back to work.

The decision for me to stay home was already subliminally made. Blindly, I went along with their plan. For my husband and his mother to get exactly what they wanted, I had to buy into their insidious form of manipulation. I eagerly walked right into the cage.

CHAPTER 10

MARRIED – 8 YEARS

It was a bright, sunny day in our small town when we decided to stop at a fast-food chain to get a quick lunch before Claire's youth soccer game. The girls were silent in the back of the van, engrossed in their electronic devices, and Carter was fast asleep in his car seat.

"Hey guys, what do you want from McDonald's?" I asked.

"Don't ask them what they want," Nick snapped. "I'll get them something from the dollar menu."

"Mommy, Mommy! I want a happy meal!" Claire yelled excitedly.

Nick turned his head to me and widened his eyes waiting for me to correct our daughter. He hung his head and breathed a heavy sigh of frustration as he pulled up to place our order. I picked up his cue and quickly diffused the excitement.

"Claire, we're just gonna get some burgers and parfaits."

"Aw, I wanted a happy meal," said Claire, disappointed.

"Seriously," he whispered harshly to keep the kids from hearing, "you don't ask kids what they want. You tell them what they're getting. You are so lucky you're pretty."

Nick ordered for the family from the dollar menu. He didn't bother asking me what I wanted. He began to order a burger for me too.

"I'd rather have a salad," I spoke up.

"A salad? Of course, you want a salad. You have to get something more expensive than everybody else in the car. Why is it I can eat something less expensive but you can't? You always get what you want though, don't you?"

He got the attention of the attendant and added a salad to the order for me.

"No, it's fine. I don't need it!" I objected, feeling guilty.

"Oh, no, no, no. I wouldn't want you to have to eat something cheap like the rest of us. I'll get you the salad, and I'll just have to work a few more years instead of retiring early. You probably want that, don't you?"

I put my head down and stared at the bowl of mixed lettuce and cherry tomatoes. My appetite was gone, and I set my plastic fork in the bowl. Nick noticed I wasn't eating.

"Well you better not waste it now that you've made me pay for it," he said.

Hesitantly, I picked up the plastic fork and forced a bite into my mouth. I swallowed the salad just like I was swallowing my voice. I didn't argue and I didn't fight back.

Watching out the window as other cars passed us on the four-lane highway, I couldn't help but wonder if this was how everyone else felt. *Was every other marriage like this? Do all husbands treat their wives this way? Do all couples argue the way we argue? Do all wives screw up as much as I do?*

Accidentally, I let out a small burp. The kids heard it and erupted in laughter. Immediate panic set in.

"Excuse me!"

I looked at Nick who was inhaling slowly with flared nostrils and pursed lips.

"You are so disgusting. I can't even look at you. I really expect more from my wife."

Ultimately, it was I who permitted Nick to treat me this way. Little by little he gained more and more control. His behavior was reprehensible. Any person would know this, but I continued to blame myself. A normal person wouldn't be so callous and manipulative as my husband, but I didn't know that. Nick wasn't normal and I was too easy to subdue. Our relationship was the perfect set up for a dictatorship and not a marriage.

CHAPTER 11

MARRIED – 8.5 YEARS

I inspected the words on my computer screen in the email from Nick. I craved his praise and acceptance, so I read it repeatedly until it was photographed into my mind. Uncertain when the next compliment would come, I wrapped his words around me like a plush duvet and nestled in comfortably.

"I am so happy when you save me money! Good job. You have really stepped it up lately and I'm noticing. I love you."

My three little children were happily playing together, squealing and giggling. Motherhood was taxing and stressful, but the email from Nick was just the morsel of motivation I needed to keep going.

Praise from him was addictive but lacking. I tackled my list of things to do and crossed off task after task. Four more hours until Nick came home to a perfectly cleaned house, fresh laundry in his drawers, weeds pulled, and a hot, home-cooked meal on the table. To avoid a lecture, I'd be sure not to call him to the table before everything was completely set and ready. Everything I did had Nick at the forefront of my mind. I knew what he hated, and I knew what would set him off. My mind was tuned to autopilot to think of Nick first.

Our marriage was not happy. I tried my best to make Nick happy, but I failed consistently. There was something seriously wrong in our marriage. He said he loved me but treated me with hate. He called me beautiful but crushed my self-confidence. He gave me false hope with not one shred of intention of treating me better. It was impossible for my husband to change and I had not the slightest idea. Each time Nick was nice to me, it was enough to keep me holding on. And every time Nick tossed me crumbs of the kudos I craved, I scrambled to collect them all.

I was pouring ice-cold milk into glasses on the dinner table when the doorbell rang. Standing on my porch was Nick's mother with a dense bouquet of multicolored carnations and a big smile.

"These are for you." She sang happily, presenting the bouquet out in front of herself.

"Me? What for?"

"Nick didn't have time to stop to get them, so he asked me to come over and bring them to you. For dealing with the guy at the hardware store and getting the money back."

"Really?"

Mike walked up behind her holding a couple of pizza boxes.

"We decided to bring dinner since Nick invited us over."

I motioned for them to come inside.

"Well, come on in," I said, "Nick will be here any minute."

"Oh, it smells so nice in here. So clean. What's that candle scent?" Barbara's nostrils flared as she happily inhaled, glancing around at my perfectly presented home.

"Thanks! It's fresh linen," I beamed. "I've been cleaning all day."

"I can see that," she said. "But looks like you forgot to dust up here."

She swiped her finger along the end of a picture frame on the wall and showed me the dust.

"Oh, thanks," I said, dryly.

Who does she think she is? Her house is nowhere near perfectly clean.

Barbara cut the ends of the flowers in the sink and filled a large glass vase with tap water and placed them on the counter. She helped me finish plating the pizza while Mike played with the grandkids in the living room. Their contagious giggles bounced throughout the house coaxing the rest of us to laugh along. Their squeals amplified when they heard their dad come home from work. He greeted them with smiles and hugs, then kissed his mother on the forehead.

"How was your day?" I asked him.

"Fine."

As I approached him for a kiss, he turned his head away from me and walked straight over to my burning candle on the counter and puffed the flame with his breath.

"We've talked about you burning candles. You know I don't like that."

"Anything interesting happen today at work?"

"I don't want to talk about work."

"I was just trying to show interest in your day and show you I care."

"Please just stop," Nick said firmly.

I tried to ignore his hatred toward me, but the tension in the air was suspended between us. The table was set, and we all sat down to eat. I passed out pizza to everyone and Barbara filled our salad bowls. I reached for the saltshaker across from Nick. He grabbed it and moved it out of my reach while tossing a sour scowl my way.

"How many times do I have to tell you that salt is bad for you?"

Darkness loomed over me. It was a sad type of veil clinging to me like a sticky spider web. All I kept thinking was what I must have done wrong to cause it. Everything seemed so positive until he came home. I wondered what I had messed up. My inward reflection sent me tumbling inside myself like Alice down the rabbit hole. *Did I forget something? Had I done something to offend him?* Continuous thoughts paraded through my mind as I tried to latch on to something I could apologize for.

During dinner, I attended to the children while Nick and his parents talked about the recent stock market prices and their lofty financial goals. My interest wasn't in our net worth or what investments were most profitable. All I cared about was why my husband seemed to dislike me so much. The abrupt change in Nick's attitude felt like I was dealing with two different people. The husband who I wanted so desperately to love me was ripped away by an apathetic stranger at my dinner table. I reflected on the love we shared at the initial stages of our relationship. I yearned to have it back.

Mindlessly, I put forkfuls of salad into my mouth. The chatter around me was as undecipherable as a foreign language. Lleyton was shoveling tiny bites of pizza into her mouth, and Claire sucked down big gulps of milk.

"Allie!" Nick said forcefully.

Startled, I dropped my fork. It hit my plate and bounced onto the floor beside me.

"What?" I looked up with wide eyes.

"I've said your name three times. Are you even listening?"

"Sorry, no. I wasn't."

He looked at his mother and shook his head back and forth then blinked hard. His palms rested on the table on either side of his plate as if he were going to stand up. Everyone was silent. Nick and I locked eyes.

"Can you not scrape your fork across your teeth every time you take a bite? And quit eating so fast. It's so rude."

Embarrassed by his request, I nodded sheepishly. I leaned over slowly to pick up my fork and gently laid it on the table.

"I'm sorry. I didn't realize."

"Thank you," he said, heaving a sigh of relief.

At this point, I just couldn't wait for his parents to go home so I could fall asleep in my bed. I was physically tired and mentally exhausted from the emotional roller coaster Nick put me on.

After dinner and a long visit from my in-laws, I changed into my pajamas and put the kids and myself to bed. A few minutes after lying there on my side, Nick came back to the room and slid under the blanket. He moved in behind me wrapping his arms around my waist. He pulled me towards him and walked his fingers up to cup my breasts. Immediately, I was filled with dread as his hard penis pushed against my back.

"I'm really tired."

"No, you're not," he said, pressing himself harder against my back.

"Nick, really. I can't. It's been a long day."

"Come on, you know you'll like it if you just give in."

I cringed. The thought of him toying with me this way made me feel sick. One minute he loved me, the next he couldn't stand me. Though I was starved for his affection, I couldn't help but believe it had little to do with me. There was no apology for his rudeness and there was no concern for me. Nick just wanted what he wanted and he usually always got it.

"I don't want to."

"Quit whining. You know you want to."

He pulled at my pajama bottoms and eased them down to my knees as he kissed the back of my neck. I squeezed my thighs together as hard as I could.

"Quit it. I mean it. I don't want to. I want to sleep." My tone became sharp and direct.

I pushed his hands away as he began fondling my bottom. He grabbed my underwear and yanked them down and held his hard bare penis against my skin. I tried to pull away from him, but he held me tighter.

"I said no!" I yelled, struggling to get out of his grip.

"Would you hold still!"

He grabbed both my wrists with one hand and tried to enter me. I kicked my legs and threw them both over the side of the bed. He released his grip and I sprung out of bed, half naked.

"I told you no!" I screamed as I backed up away from the bed.

"What is your problem? I'm just trying to have sex with my wife."

"No, you're not! You're trying to rape me."

Nick laughed at me and fell back onto his pillow with his hands behind his head.

"Are you kidding me? You can't rape your wife," he scoffed.

"Yes, you can! I said no and you kept going. If I say no, I mean no. You do this all the time and I don't like it."

"Husbands and wives are supposed to have sex. You need to think about how you make me feel when you reject me like this. It doesn't feel very good. How would you feel if I turned you down as often as you turn me down? Huh?"

I ignored the question. A fight wasn't worth it at this point. He rarely showed interest in me and even withheld simple types of affection like a kiss or a hug. He was instilling insecurity in me through withholding and I wasn't even aware. After the highs and lows of the day, his expectations were for me to attend to his needs no matter what. He coerced and guilted me into sexual acts to get what he wanted. Nick lacked much in the way of common sense, but where it was lacking, his evil skill of wily wrongdoing rewarded him.

None of this was or is okay. Ever. His hypocrisy was shining brightly. I closed my eyes to it avoiding a battle I knew I couldn't win. Nick flipped over, pulled the blanket over him and left me alone, before leaving me with one final thought.

"You never put me first. I fully expect you to wake me in the middle of the night to give me a blow job. You owe me and you know it."

CHAPTER 12

MARRIED – 9 YEARS

Our sweet little dog, Worthy, spent the first seven years of his life in our home. With the addition of three children paired with a new stressor of building a new home on our dream property, things changed dramatically for Worthy. He had taken a backseat.

"Worthy! Stop licking the carpet," I'd snap at him.

He would stop for a minute or two and go right back to licking incessantly. His habit of licking the floor was beginning to grate on my nerves. It was constant. He was bored.

"When we move into the new house, Worthy has to be an outdoor dog. I cannot have him wearing down our brand-new carpet at the new house," I declared.

Nick never challenged me or disagreed. He didn't seem to care either way.

After several trying months of custom home building, we finally moved into our new house. It was summertime and Worthy seemed to enjoy the outdoors. He had acres to run, play, and explore. He trekked the woods and fields, dug for moles, and chased after rabbits and birds.

He seemed happy. But as winter started to creep in, I started to worry about our sweet dog. It was getting bitterly cold outside, and I didn't want Worthy to suffer. I helped Nick make him a little doghouse, but it still broke my heart knowing Worthy was alone outside in the elements. It broke my heart watching him shiver at the door.

"We need to bring him inside," I said. "It's going to get really cold tonight. I don't want him to be an outdoor dog anymore. I don't care if he licks the carpet. He needs to be in here with us."

Since Nick never seemed to care, I truly thought he was going to say yes.

"Absolutely not," he said.

"What? Why?" I asked, completely shocked at his response.

"You made the choice to turn him into an outdoor dog, now you can live with it."

"That's not fair! I changed my mind. I can change my mind. I don't want him out there alone. He was fine in the summer and fall, but he's going to freeze out there. It's too cold for him to be outside all alone."

"Sorry. If you didn't want him to be an outdoor dog, you should have let him come in to begin with. This is on you. He has a doghouse. He'll be fine. Dogs have been outdoor animals for centuries. He'll survive."

The guilt was overwhelming. This was my fault. If I had never made the decision to put him outside, I wouldn't be fighting Nick to bring him back in.

"Please! I can't stand it. He's a good dog. He spent years in our old house. He will be fine in here too. We can just put him in the unfinished basement." I tried to appeal to Nick's logic.

"You need help. I don't have time for this garbage. Worthy isn't coming in because you chose to put him out, remember?"

Nick's words cut me.

"I know, but now I don't want it that way anymore. I can change my mind."

Nick disagreed.

"Oh, no you can't. There's always some kind of drama with you. I'm not going to let you go back on your word. You made your bed, now you lie in it."

"You are so mean," I yelled. "This is animal cruelty! He is our family dog!"

"You know, there really is no love in your voice right now," he said calmly. "You know this isn't animal cruelty. Nobody thinks that way except you. And I really don't appreciate you calling me names. You should look at yourself and your own issues, because there are a lot."

I looked at Worthy from the kitchen window. He stared at me shivering with his wiry gray fur sprinkled in snow. I took an armful of extra blankets outside to stuff into and around his doghouse. I coaxed him into it, hoping it was warm enough for him to be comfortable. He followed in as I ordered. I pet him on the head and warm tears rolled down my face against the icy wind biting at my cheeks. I grabbed an electric heating pad to put inside the doghouse, and when Nick saw me with it, he demanded I put it back.

"You will not put that out there. We will have major problems if you try to put it out there for him." His threats felt like thick ropes tightening on my wrists. I obeyed and took the heating pad back inside.

"I'm sorry little buddy," I cried. "I'm so sorry."

My sweet and wonderful pup must have understood my sadness. I don't know how, but even though I allowed and enabled his neglect, he still loved me unconditionally. A type of love I'd never receive from Nick.

CHAPTER 13

MARRIED – 9.5 YEARS

"I have an idea," Nick said, pulling up a seat behind me at the kitchen island.

"Oh yeah? What's that?" I asked while flipping pancakes.

"After breakfast, let's take a drive out to that new nursery you were telling me about and get some vegetable plants for the garden."

I spun around holding the spatula like a magic wand in the air. My eyes were wide and my mouth agape.

"Really?! Are you serious?"

"Yeah," he shrugged. "It's Mother's Day and I thought you'd like to go."

"Yes! I'd love that."

Bashfully, I walked over to my husband and draped my arms around his neck to show my appreciation for his offer. I leaned in to kiss him and he turned his head away, forcing my lips against the sandpaper stubble on his cheek. I leaned my head the other way, continuing to try to meet our lips, and he turned again and again until I finally gave up.

"Why won't you kiss me?" I whined.

He looked over my shoulder and motioned to the stovetop.

"Your pancakes are gonna burn."

Jolted from my self-pity, I flew back to the griddle to rescue my Mother's Day breakfast. *Thank goodness, not burned.*

"They're fine. Don't worry," I assured him.

"Well it wouldn't be the first time you ever burned something," he laughed.

"At least I actually cook. You can't even make yourself sandwich!"

It was quiet as I flipped the pancakes over one by one. It was clear he didn't find my banter amusing by his silence. After a few minutes he interjected, refusing to let me have the last word.

"Why do you always have to be so feisty? I was making a joke, and then you go on attack and make fun of me. Real nice."

He crossed his arms across his chest. Defensively, I piped up to plead my case.

"I wasn't attacking you at all. I was joking with you like you joke with me."

He shook his head back and forth slowly in disbelief at what I had just said. He scoffed.

"Well, the fact is, you actually have burned things before. Many times. So, what I said to you in a teasing manner actually has some weight. I know how to make a sandwich and you know it. I might not cook, but cooking's not my job. Just like your job isn't to go to work every day and make money."

"I'm sorry. I didn't mean to be rude."

"You never mean to do anything. You always fight me on everything, even when I'm joking."

Nick pushed himself away from the island and left the kitchen somberly. While he was gone, I reflected on what he said. *I am feisty sometimes. I wasn't trying to hurt his feelings. He was just being playful. I should be more careful with my words next time.*

The kids were lively during breakfast, but it was silent as death between Nick and me. He sulked through the meal, and I was avoiding possible tension so he didn't cancel our trip to go plant shopping. I was careful not to upset him again so we could pretend nothing happened and maintain a temporary sense of normalcy. This was typically a pretty reliable plan: Avoid waking the sleeping giant by tiptoeing around.

By the time we got home from shopping, the van loaded with young vegetable and herb plants, Nick and I were operating normally. He took responsibility for getting out the rototiller and I began moving the plants, seeds, and gardening supplies to the garden. Nick laid out the plan where the plants would go and physically labored with me to get them in the ground. He directed the order of operations and I obeyed. There were times I disagreed with his plan or what to do next, but it wasn't worth bringing up. There were instances it made more sense for him to fetch something from the garage, but I did as directed to avoid being accused of laziness or lacking cooperation. It was Mother's Day after all and I wanted to enjoy spending the day outdoors, doing what I liked and watching my kids run around the yard.

Touching the warm earth in my bare hands, made me feel connected to something. Carefully placing those delicate roots into the ground gave me a sense of nurture. Watching their tiny leaves flutter in the breeze gave me hope for their strength and growth. Each plant required something different. Each one needed special care to help it flourish. We would tend to them meticulously, removing weeds that choked out their nutrients. We would water them regularly, allowing them the opportunity to produce a fruitful harvest. We would protect them from insects and other wildlife whose only intent was to destroy the plant for its own survival. We would provide them a safe and sunny place to live and in return, they provided us with a bountiful crop.

"This looks great," he said.

We both stood back and admired what we had just accomplished through the day.

"It really does," I replied.

He smiled at me. I smiled back.

"You've got some dirt on your face," he laughed, reaching out to wipe my forehead.

"Oh, on my face? I think I have it everywhere." I laughed, inspecting my hands and my clothing.

"I'll pick up the tools, why don't you go ahead and get a shower?"

"Are you sure? I don't mind helping clean up," I said.

"I'm sure. It's Mother's Day. I got it. Just don't let the water run so long like you normally do. You can't possibly need more than ten minutes."

Hesitantly, I agreed and went inside to clean myself up in the shower. The entire time I felt guilty that Nick was doing all of the outdoor clean up on his own. From the bathroom window I watched him picking up tools and empty plant containers and couldn't shake the uneasiness within me. It was confusing. *He is being so nice to me now. Did he feel guilty for being rude earlier at breakfast? Is there some other motive for why he's cleaning up on his own? Will I owe him something in return later?* I was so uncomfortable just taking a shower to relax and had no idea why.

As the years passed, each growing season in the garden declined. Instead of the plants flourishing, they decayed. Nick added more and more work to my list of chores. He expanded the size of the garden. He added blueberry bushes, several rows of blackberries and raspberries, fruit trees, asparagus and raised beds full of herbs and root vegetables. My work outside became more and more difficult for me to keep up with. Even though I didn't work outside of the home, I could not keep up with the multitude of responsibilities Nick kept piling on. Stress crept in, anxiety was overwhelming my emotions and it showed up in anger directed at my children.

The weeding was out of control, the pests and insects were chewing holes in the leaves and the fruits were rotting on the ground below. The beautiful garden we had started had gone from something full of life to a graveyard of sick, dying and dead foliage. The bright green leaves turned to brown. The luscious stems were drained of moisture, leaving brittle sticks barely able to stand upright. Powdery mildew spread virally over the broad leaves shielding them from their precious sunlight. And sprinkled in between were the multitude of weeds, spreading like an infectious disease over the earth.

The kids and I spent hours in the scorching heat pulling weeds and stuffing them into buckets. They whined to go inside, I whined because I needed more help. *God, I hate this.* As much as I wanted to break down and cry, I kept going with dirt-caked hands. Gnats flew at my eyes, sweat rolled down my forehead and my back ached. Nick was going to need to see evidence of our work when he got home so I did as much as I could. *Hurry up. Pull faster. Pull more.* It was futile though. As quickly as I pulled weeds, more were sprouting. Regardless of how much or little produce I brought in, it still needed to be washed, prepared, frozen, or canned. Every bit of it was daunting to me and I knew I would soon give up.

Initially, it broke my heart to watch my precious plants wither away. No matter how hard I tried to save them, I just couldn't do it. It was overwhelming and out of control. Being the only one tending to them was discouraging and sad. Each time Nick would come home and inspect my work in the garden, I would be overcome with anxiety. His criticism of my failure to thoroughly weed distressed me. He brought me to the dying plot of land and pointed out how wasteful I was for not getting to the harvest quickly enough and allowing the crops to die. The criticism stung like the cuts on my hands as I ripped sharp blades of grass from the dirt. The garden would never be good enough for Nick. I would never be good enough for him either.

"You keep telling me all the things I do wrong and you hardly ever tell me what I do right. Don't you realize you just keep chipping away at me and eventually there won't be anything left."

He dismissed my feelings. He told me I needed to toughen up and take criticism better. He said I was too sensitive and needed to suck it up. But what I really needed was more love and positivity. I needed encouragement and support from my husband.

Over time, my love for gardening turned sour. It was no longer enjoyable to me. It was only a massive headache I began to dread each and every day. It eventually got to the point of me longing to rip every last plant out of the ground, toss them in a roaring fire and watch them singe and crackle under the heat. *I don't care anymore,* I thought, as I imagined the dead plants shrinking and turning to ash as the smoke billowed around. The garden was a burden in more ways than one, and instead of suffering through the insurmountable chore, I simply decided it wasn't worth it.

CHAPTER 14

MARRIED – 10 YEARS

"Daddy," our middle daughter yelled from the back of the van, "will there be sharks at the beach?!"

Nick glanced at her through his rearview mirror.

"No, silly girl. Sharks only live in the ocean, not on the beach!" he laughed.

I looked at him with love. *He's a good dad. Playful.* This is what I liked about him.

"Da-Deeeee," she said, huffing with frustration, "I mean in the ocean!"

"Oh, the ocean is what you meant?!" he said, feigning confusion.

"Are you just being silly now, Dad?" she asked, suspiciously.

Nick looked over at me and we both let out some laughter.

"Yes, Lleyton, Dad is just being silly," I interjected.

"Well!? Is there or not? Tell me!" she demanded.

"Yes, there are sharks in the ocean where we're are going."

"See, Claire?! Told you!" she shouted at her sister.

"So what? I don't even like sharks. I like seahorses!"

The girls began their banter and little Carter was asleep upright in his car seat. I looked back at all of them, excited to be on our way to family vacation in Florida. We had been on the road for a few hours. The kids were behaving well, traffic was light, and we were making decent time.

"Which way am I going next?" Nick asked anxiously.

I stared at the moving road map on the navigation system between my hands and placed my bare feet on the dashboard. Nick leaned into the passenger side, placed his hand over my shins and pushed down on my legs, forcing my feet to the floorboard.

"I don't know. The arrows are pointing this way, but I'm not sure which road to take." My heart began to race. We were approaching a rather complex set of roads dividing in the heart of a major city.

"How can you not know when to tell me to turn? I need to know now or we're going to miss it!"

I had an overwhelming sense of anxiety hit me. My chest felt heavy and my breathing became more rapid. *He's getting upset. Focus Allie.*

"I don't know, it's really confusing in this area. I'm sorry! I don't know!"

"Seriously?! It's very easy. You just look at the map and it will tell you where to go. I need to know right now!"

I couldn't speak. I was frozen with anxiety and didn't want to say the wrong thing. He chose a path. He had to. He waited as long as possible and whipped the wheel to the left. A driver in his blind spot leaned on his horn while trying to avoid slamming into the side of our van. I braced myself, gripping the passenger handle.

"Don't act scared because of my driving now. That was your fault and now we're lost. Great job. All I asked you to do was tell me which road to turn onto before we got to it, and you couldn't even do that right. I cannot believe this. Do you even know how frustrating this is for me? Do you even care? You should know because I tell you all the time how inefficient your driving is. Do you do this stuff on purpose to upset me?"

Nick shook his head back and forth while focusing on the road ahead. I could feel his disdain for me like a backhand slap to my face.

"You just added thirty more minutes to our drive. Do you realize that?"

I felt guilty which was his intent. He needed someone to blame and it was always me.

"But the arrow is pointing one way and the road looks like it goes another way."

"That is not true. Why are you lying now? It's bad enough you got us lost. Now you are lying about it?"

"I'm not lying! I was confused!"

I felt my eyes get hot and a lump forming at the back of my throat.

"You seriously cannot be this stupid. I know you're not this stupid. Are you? It's really simple. All you have to do is look at the map and tell me which way to go."

His words reeked with condescension. I was silent as we continued to drive, holding back tears and biting at the cuticle skin around my thumbnail.

He focused on the road ahead. His hands gripped the wheel so tightly his knuckles were white. He looked at me with squinted eyes.

"Stop biting your nails! Such a gross habit."

I shoved my hand under my thigh.

"Please just tell me where to go next and do it right so we don't get lost again."

"I never said I wasn't going to help you. I was trying to help you before you got mad at me."

"Well you're going to have to do better then. Because whatever *that* was, it was no help at all. Where do I go next?"

I summed up as much courage as I could to defend myself and spoke calmly in reply.

"I don't really feel like navigating if you're going to blame me for getting lost and make me feel dumb. It was a simple mistake and it's not a big deal. We can just go another way."

"What? Who else am I supposed to blame? You were the one navigating. I can't help it if you feel dumb. I'm not trying to make you feel dumb, but maybe there's a reason you feel that way. Maybe you should look at yourself? I mean, where is your mind at? I don't even want you to say sorry. I want you to not mess up. Sorry doesn't save us thirty minutes, because now we have to go another route, and we're going to be on the road even longer."

He rambled. I was silent.

"I have been driving for four hours already," he said, "and you don't seem to care at all. My back hurts and you don't even think about me. How am I supposed to think you care about me when these things happen?"

His voice trailed off and I interrupted.

"If you want to pull over, I can drive. I'm happy to drive."

"Ha! No thank you, I'd rather get there alive, and that won't happen with you driving."

"Okay then, fine. You can just navigate yourself. I'm not doing it anymore."

"No. I am driving and I can't be worried about the GPS. You have to do it. I need to focus on driving and being safe. You just have to do it and do it right."

"I'm not doing it!" I yelled.

The kids began to cry in the back of the van.

"Mommy, stop yelling."

"Now look at what you did. That's just great. Great way to start out our vacation."

Intense sadness overwhelmed me. In my best effort to keep from crying I swallowed as hard as I could and squeezed my eyes shut. Nick was so hurtful. I knew how he was treating me was wrong, yet I still felt everything was my fault. It really made no difference if I made valid points or gave legitimate reasoning why he wasn't behaving properly toward me. Nick would find a way to ensure I knew my place far beneath him.

"You will do it. You don't have a choice," he said.

I really didn't feel as if I had a choice. Even though I wanted so desperately to fight him, I was confident it would just make things worse. The pain he inflicted on my psyche and my soul was too much to bear for a lengthy amount of time. So, I decided to hold the GPS device and be the navigator like he wanted. Without sense, I had bent to his will.

The remainder of our drive was pretty quiet and uneventful. My focus was avoiding another argument like the one we just had. *Don't mess up Allie. Focus on the map. Concentrate.* In previous instances like this, I would make even more errors. It seemed like the more I tried not to screw up, the more mistakes I made. It didn't matter where or when, if I knew the scrutiny was on me, there would be a mistake. Excess pressure from him never improved my performance. The extra stress he put on me caused me to crumble. *Please let us get there soon. One more hour left in our drive.* I couldn't wait to get out of the van and meet the rest of the family. Nick wasn't quite as mean to me when other people were around. People around us always served as a comfortable buffer for me, so I always preferred the company of others versus alone time with him.

Finally, we arrived, pulling up beside the beach house his parents rented for the week.

"Figures, everyone else gets the good parking spots. You'd think my brother would be nice enough to give me the parking spot after I let him borrow my truck last week. People can be so ungrateful. I guess we'll park on the street."

He complained incessantly. Not just about me and my faults, but others and theirs too. It was emotionally draining and mentally exhausting.

My mouth was shut tightly. There was no need for me to say anything to open up an opportunity for Nick to start lecturing me again. We unloaded our luggage and greeted the rest of the family who were changing into bathing suits and loading up items to take to the beach.

The kids were anxious to play with their cousins from the long drive, and I was anxious to talk to anyone other than Nick.

"Mommy! Can we go? Can we go?" Claire asked hopefully, pulling at my shirt.

"Honey, let me ask your dad," I said.

Nick looked over at me with a blank stare, awaiting the question.

"Can we go to the beach with everybody?" I asked.

"Yeah, let's get changed. We'll be a little behind them, but the kids need to stretch their legs."

I was immediately relieved. The kids and I rushed around as quickly as possible, digging through our suitcases for towels and sunscreen. I went through my mental list of things to bring so I didn't forget something. Within minutes, we were ready and out the door.

The yellow sun blazed overhead, burning the sand beneath our feet. A flock of seagulls hovered overhead and dove towards the beach looking for food. The ocean waves were slapping at the coast emitting smells of salt and seaweed all around us. The kids set up a spot to dig holes in the sand as we watched them playing against a seascape backdrop.

"This is the life, isn't it?" I said to Nick as we laid our towels on some empty beach chairs under the shade. Sometimes if I was lucky, Nick would forget about our arguments pretty quickly if I could distract him. The warm breeze caressed my skin and the shadows of palm leaves danced on my body. The kids' laughter was muffled by the waves crashing as they played in the sand.

"Yeah, this is really nice," he said, pulling out from the beach bag a Dan Brown novel to read.

"Hey guys! Look what I got for you!" My sister-in-law, Jenny, sang as she handed Nick and I each a plastic cup with a red and yellow mixed frozen cocktail.

"These look great! Thanks! Where's Adam?" I asked as I put the cup to my lips.

"He's coming," she waved her finger down towards the beach. "He's getting a few extra drinks at that cabana up there for whoever wants them."

My sister-in-law plopped down on the chair next to me and took a long sip of her fruity concoction then twisted the base of her cup down into the sand.

"This is going to be such a fun vacation!" I stretched out my lean, tanned body and tilted my head back towards the sky.

"Allie, not to be a weirdo or anything, but damn your body looks good," Jenny said.

"What?! Look at you! You look amazing!" I replied.

"No, I mean it! Do you know how lucky you are," Jenny said to Nick. "Look at her, she looks ten years younger than her age!"

"You're sweet, Jen, thanks."

She knew I'd been working out, and she knew Nick didn't really notice. She was the closest person to me in the family. We leaned on each other when we argued with our husbands. We talked frequently and enjoyed each other's company. She was my best friend.

Nick reached out his hand and laid it on my thigh. He gently stroked my skin. It felt nice. He toyed with the string bikini tie at my hip. I paid no attention. I was lost in my tropical bliss.

"Uh oh," he said as he yanked the string holding my bottoms on. It unraveled, revealing my bare hip.

"Nick!" I laughed, grabbing the tie. "You are such a child!"

He shrugged and winked at me.

"I'll show you I'm not a child later on tonight."

"Gross! I don't need to hear that!" Jenny laughed.

I fastened the strings back into a bow. Nick set his book down and stood up from his chair.

"Come on, let's go get in the water!"

Jenny and I both agreed and, as I led the way, Nick yanked the string at the back of my bikini top and sprinted for the ocean. I grabbed my breasts to keep from exposing myself and ran after him. I met him in the waves, and he playfully picked me up and cradled me like a small child in his arms.

"Tie this back for me?" I laughed.

"Nope. I think it looks better like this."

I giggled, soaking up the attention from him. He hoisted me up and tossed me into the warm water. Jenny was standing there as I surfaced.

"Turn around," she laughed. "I'll tie it for you."

Nick was standing with the sun at his back. The light sparkled against the waves and for a few seconds I stood entranced with the goodness of him. He was brilliant, moving with the gentle rise and fall of the water. He stared directly into my eyes, and I saw the man I had fallen in love with so many years earlier. *Why couldn't every day be like this? Why, at minimum, couldn't most days be like this?* Pure joy permeated through me, and the world could have disappeared, and I wouldn't have noticed. But the feeling was fleeting. As quickly as it entered, it would exit. It was a shiny, red balloon, and its string slipped right through my fingers.

After the quick dip in the water, we got back to our chairs where Nick's brother, Adam, was straddling a seat with four cups of liquor in front of him.

"I was wondering where you guys went. Was about to keep these all to myself."

He carefully handed out the cups to each of us.

"Good Lord, Adam, we haven't even finished our first drinks yet! We'll be hammered before noon!" I said.

Adam playfully squirted a lime wedge at me, spraying little droplets onto my face. I winced.

"We're on vacation. That's the point!" He laughed.

"Um, this is way too big," Jenny objected, staring at the large cup full of liquor.

"That's what she said," Nick joked, attempting his best impression of Michael Scott, from The Office. We all let out a little laugh and I rolled my eyes.

"What I want to know," I added, "is who is SHE and why is SHE always making dirty jokes?!"

Adam and Jenny laughed a little harder at my humor, but Nick didn't find it amusing. Then again, he never really did find me very funny. It never stopped me from trying, though.

My in-laws treated the entire family to a vacation every year. They'd been doing this since their boys were very little. They were wealthy, but lived below their means on a day-to-day basis. They relished in spoiling their family and themselves when it came to quality time together. No expense was spared on elaborate all-inclusive resorts, enormous beach homes, and excursions. Clear expectations of all of our attendance on these trips were laid out in advance. This was what they did, and we were all expected to go.

"Meemaw, Meemaw! Come look at our moat!" one of the kids yelled from the beach.

Barbara sat under a shade umbrella, concentrating on a crossword puzzle. Her long-sleeved cover up hid her old crepe skin she'd earned from years of sun worshipping in her youth. She looked up from the book and slid the pen between the pages.

"I'm coming!" she shouted as she walked toward the grandkids ferociously digging in the sand. Their tiny hands, like shovels, flung wet sand overhead and all around them. I hopped up from my chair and skipped toward them, kicking up the loose powder as I approached her.

"Hey, thank you so much for bringing us here," I said.

"Oh, you're welcome, dear."

There was a peaceful silence between us as we both took in the sights and smells of the coast. She smiled, watching all of her grandchildren playing together in the sand.

"Gosh, I'm starting to get hungry," I said.

"Oh, that reminds me! Tell everybody Mike and I planned a moonlight seafood dinner on the beach for everyone," she beamed with pride.

"Wow! On the beach?! That sounds amazing!"

I looked over at the kids, and Lleyton's curly locks were sticking to her sun-kissed cheeks with salt water and sand.

"Meemaw, we're having seafood dinner on the beach tonight!?" she asked hopefully.

"Yes! Won't it be fun?"

"Do we get to catch our own fish too?"

Barbara and I laughed at her innocence.

"No, silly," I said. "They bring the food out to us!"

The older kids giggled. Embarrassed, Lleyton ran over to me, wrapped her arms around my leg and buried her face into my thigh. I stroked the top of her head, trying to wipe some of the sand out of her hair.

"Oh LeyLey, stop pouting," Barbara said, crouching down to her height.

"She's fine, just embarrassed," I told her, trying not to make it a big deal.

"You know, you can't always coddle her like this."

"Barbara," I gasped overdramatically, "Nick told me when he was little, he was a cry-baby. He said he would get mad and quit playing with his friends, and you would sit and read books with him after he threw a fit."

"That's not the same thing."

"Yes, it is."

"No, it isn't. I was showing my son love and affection, and I know you know how important it is to raise a well-adjusted child into adulthood."

"Maybe you should have told him to go back outside and quit being a sore loser. You were just teaching him he could behave however he wanted with no consequences. In fact, with rewards, from you!"

Nick's mom was like a mother to me. She and I were very close. The further my mother was pushed aside, the closer Barbara and I became. She straightened her posture and looked away from me, fixing her sights on a tiny boat in the distance. The rims of her eyelids under her crooked lashes were pink. Her eyes became glossy with tears, and she blinked a few times refusing to let them fall.

"Well, you married him," she shot back at me. "You must not think he's too bad of a guy."

"That isn't what I meant."

As I attempted to clarify, she cut me off midway.

"It's okay. Don't worry about it. I'm sure Nick will tell you he had a wonderful upbringing and a very happy childhood."

I suddenly felt a wave of guilt rush over me. My stomach sank deeper into my belly. *Why did I say anything? I should have just kept my mouth shut.*

"I'm sorry. I didn't mean to insinuate anything."

"Mmm hmm. It's fine."

Barbara forced a smile and nodded her head. She briskly walked back to her lounge chair in the shade. I stayed behind and played with the kids for a while deliberately keeping my distance from her. She wasn't one to outwardly show anger or frustration and it was never my intention to offend or hurt her. My inward reflection was halted when I heard my name being shouted by my husband's deep recognizable tone. I turned to see him, Adam and Jenny excitedly waving me in.

"What's going on?" I asked as I neared them.

"Tequila tasting at 11:30 at the bar down there and a bubble party at 12," Nick said.

"Oh no, no, no," I laughed, backing away from the group a few steps. "You know how much I hate tequila," I pretended to gag.

"Aw, come on, babe, you'll be fine. It's just a tasting. I just wanna have fun with you."

Nick reached for my waist and pulled me into his body. I inhaled the coconut and pineapple scents from the sunscreen on his bare chest.

Jenny was pulling her glossy, black hair into a messy knot on the top of her head.

"Just go with us," she said. "I can't be with these two idiots by myself."

"Alright, I'll go," I said, covering my mouth with both hands, "but I'm not drinking that stuff."

Nick lifted me up and spun me around.

"Geez, what do you weigh? 100 pounds soaking wet?" he said, laughing.

I enjoyed his flattery. The sun was shining, we were on a beautiful, tropical vacation, and life was good. I yearned for more of this every single day. I hoped for this feeling of joy. He reminded me so much of the 19 year old I'd first met. *I wish he were like this all the time.* Glimpses like these are what kept me hanging on so tightly. *I want this forever.*

CHAPTER 15

MARRIED — 10.5 YEARS

"Happy Birthday." I whispered as I nuzzled my face into my little boy's soft cheek. I kissed him gently and he threw his arms around my neck.

"Happy birt-day, Mommy!" he said.

"It's not my birthday, silly boy!" I laughed, and Carter let out a high-pitched squeal as I tickled his neck.

"Daddy has a surprise for you today," I said.

His pretty eyes cast downward, and his little rounded shoulders slumped.

"What's the matter, sweetie?"

"Daddy's gonna make me tell on you."

"What do you mean, bud?"

"To get my supwise. He says I get a supwise when I tell him when you speed in the caw."

"What? When I speed?"

"Mm hm. And I don't want to tell on you."

Involving our child as a spy on his own mother was despicable behavior. Rage was vibrating inside me.

"Well, don't worry about it honey. This is your birthday present, and Daddy wants to take us all to the creek to play and look for snakes and crawfish. Would you like to go to the creek today?"

"Yes!" His eyes widened and he sat up in bed tossing his little stuffed dog in the air.

"I get dwessed wight now!"

The excitement in him warmed my heart. He bounced eagerly on the mattress, and his smile spread from ear to ear. It was almost enough to quell my anger.

"Well, hold on, buddy, we have to eat breakfast first. I made French toast and bacon."

"Oh yummy! Tank you, Mommy!" he shouted. His voice trailed off down the hallway as his little bare feet slapped across the hardwood.

"Daddy, Daddy! I go to da cweek!"

Nick shot me an evil glare. He scowled at me as he replied to Carter.

"Yes, we are. But Mommy just ruined my surprise for you because I wanted to tell you my plans."

I poured milk into Nick's glass. He shook his head and looked at his breakfast plate.

"Did you tell me not to say anything?"

He interrupted me in mid-sentence and slammed his fork down on the table.

"You knew I wanted to tell him. Don't act like you didn't. Now you're trying to take credit for my surprise."

The kids were shoveling syrup-smothered bites into their mouths and didn't appear to notice our argument. I lowered my head.

"I'm sorry. I didn't mean to."

I turned to put the milk away, remembering to put it on the correct shelf where Nick insisted I place it.

"You know, I really expect more from my wife and mother of my children," Nick said after swallowing a large bite of the gooey bread.

"Also, don't ever serve powdered sugar with French toast again. It's not healthy. Syrup is fine."

"Why? When I was a kid we used powdered sugar."

Claire leaned across the table and grabbed the bag. Nick grabbed it and pulled it away from her before she could dump any onto her plate. She released her grip and slowly sat down in her chair.

"We do not eat powdered sugar with our French toast. It is not healthy."

Comparing both nutrition labels on the syrup and the sugar, I discovered the syrup was worse. I wanted to prove him wrong.

"Actually, there's more calories and sugar in the syrup than in the sugar. So, the powdered sugar is better."

I was proud of myself for pointing out his lies. It wasn't often I won arguments and debates with him and when I had actual evidence, it felt even more satisfying.

"See?" I said, holding out the half full bag in one hand the plastic syrup container in the other.

"It's not healthier. I don't need to look at the labels. Just put it away."

"I'm not lying, Nick! Look!"

My excitement was bursting out of me. He was not amused. He looked me directly in the eyes, unblinking, refusing to look at the nutrition labels.

"It's not healthy. We do not eat powdered sugar with our French toast. Do not serve it this way again."

The imbalance of power between us left me feeling powerless in my own home. Ignoring the facts to maintain a sense of superiority sent anger rushing through my veins. *God you are such an asshole! Why can't you just choke on your breakfast and die?!* I wouldn't even call 911 if he started choking. I'd just watch the fear flash in his eyes as he panicked and collapsed from suffocation. Such injustice was like watching a criminal get away with a crime. Continuing to argue was useless, as I would be accused of picking fights. Pointing out the facts would open up opportunities for him to attack my character and motives in the marriage. My options were limited. I had to agree or shut up, unless I wanted the condescension to continue.

The rest of breakfast was quiet between us. He talked to the kids about getting nets and buckets together and, after I cleaned up the mess, the four of them hurried to get the supplies. We walked down our long driveway to the creek by the road as I trailed behind them all.

"Okay guys, let's try to lift up some of these rocks around here. We should be able to find some water snakes. They like to hide here because the rocks get warm in the sun."

Nick instructed the kids like a biology teacher on a field trip. I felt like an outcast. It was as if I was watching their life, but I wasn't a part of it. *Why didn't he include me? Why am I an outsider in my own family?* I was a ghost. I imagined picking up a rather large rock and slamming it over his head as he crouched looking for snakes. Then I imagined my children screaming in horror and swiftly pushed the thought out of my mind. *Why do I hate him so much?*

The kids lifted rocks, and I took pictures of the three of them and their father together. I captured their smiles and joy while they bumbled around on the rocks and splashed in the warm water. It really looked picture perfect. Everyone in the photo was happy, but I couldn't have been sadder behind the lens.

"Look," Claire yelled, "I found one! I found a snake!"

She pointed at the creek bed and her eyes lit up. We all stumbled over the rocks to where she stood. She was crouched down, balancing a large, flat rock on its edge. The little, brown snake was perfectly still and coiled up.

"Wow, she's really pretty," Lleyton mused, "can we touch her?"

She looked at her dad anxious and hopeful. Her big brown eyes were shining with curiosity.

"No, let's just leave it alone. This is its natural habitat. When we care about animals, we don't hurt them. Let's just look at the snake, and then put the rock back gently, okay? Then we can look for more."

"Okay, Dad," the kids agreed in unison while staring at the little snake under the rock.

As much as I felt excluded, I was still proud of the lesson Nick was teaching our children. They would learn to care about animals and respect nature. Even in anger and sadness, I couldn't deny he was being a good role model. He always put the kids before me which I tried to convince him wasn't good for the kids to see. He vehemently disagreed with me when I approached him with an article asserting spouses should put each other first, even before their kids. But that wasn't the way of it in our home. Nick came first, then the kids and then me.

After our creek adventure was finished, a violent storm with high winds and heavy rain briefly passed overhead. Once the skies cleared, my sister-in-law, Amy, who lived nearby, called me and said she found a nest of baby squirrels on the ground and asked me for help.

"Bring them here and I'll see what I can do."

I wasn't an animal expert, but I was an animal lover, and I was very resourceful. She handed me the three little babies in a shoebox filled with leaves. Their eyes were unopened slits. Their tails, sleek like a rat's. These were very young squirrels, and I was concerned because they had no mother. I placed the box on our kitchen counter and the kids hopped up on chairs and stools to get a look. They were so frail and tiny. I couldn't believe they survived the fall out of the tree.

"You cannot keep those in here," Nick said as he came over to inspect them.

"What? Why? What am I going to do then?" I asked.

"Put them back outside. Let nature take its course," he said.

"No! If I put them back outside, they will be eaten alive by some wild animal. I'm not going to lay three helpless, little animals outside to die. No."

"I disagree with this. They're just stupid squirrels, and I am not gonna be a part of this. Don't let taking care of these things take away from the time you should be spending doing work around here."

He used that phrase often with me. *"It's a squirrel." "It's a bird." "It's a dog."* He attempted to simplify and devalue the life of the animal. I rolled my eyes behind his back and went to the Internet to learn how to take care of the helpless creatures.

I kept them alive for a week with cat's milk and warmth and was able to find a local squirrel rehabilitator who would raise and release them back into the wild. Nick scoffed to my face and told me how ridiculous I was. But I ignored him. It wasn't in my nature or my instincts to let these animals die. My efforts made a difference. It gave me pride to know they would grow up and scamper among the trees because I didn't leave them outside to die.

The day I arrived home from dropping off the baby squirrels with the rehabilitator, I noticed Worthy was limping along the driveway as I was pulling in. He was clearly hurt. Upon checking him, I found a sizable gash on his belly exposing flesh with the likeness of raw chicken breast.

"Oh buddy, what happened to you?"

Worthy laid down on the floor, exhausted and weak. There was no question he needed stitches. I ran inside the house and called Nick at work.

"Nick, I have to take Worthy in to see a vet. He's hurt really bad."

"Lee," he said.

"What?" I asked, confused.

"He's hurt bad-'ly', you didn't say it right. It's an adverb."

"Nick! I don't care about your stupid adverbs right now, I care about our dog and stitching the gash on his belly."

"Absolutely not. Do you have any idea how much it'll cost?"

"No, but he's hurt bad and it could get infected," I pleaded my argument hoping he would budge.

"Lee," Nick said dryly.

My frustration was almost to a boiling point.

"Nick, I don't care about adverbs! Worthy is hurt!"

Why his focus was on anything but our pet needing immediate help baffled me. I wanted to reach through the phone and smack him.

"What is wrong with you?! Our dog needs stitches! I am taking him to the vet!" I screamed.

"No, you are not. I'll take him out into the back yard and shoot him when I get home from work tonight."

"You will do what?! Are you out of your mind?" I shrieked. "Worthy is our dog! You can't just shoot him!"

"Worthy is *a* dog," he corrected me, "and if you think I won't put a fifty-cent bullet in his head as opposed to spending a couple hundred on stitches, you're wrong."

My heart sank into my stomach. The bony fingers of fear constricted my neck, choking my throat and forcing tears from my eyes. I whimpered through the phone trying to hold back my tears.

"I really can't do this right now. I have work to do. I told you my decision and if you take him to the vet, you and I are going to have a big problem."

Nick hung up the phone, and I was frozen with shock and fear. I thought about ways I could take the dog without Nick knowing. I considered asking for help from a family member but if I asked for help, they would know what kind of monster Nick truly was. I had to protect Nick's image so I could protect my dog and myself. I had to find a way to handle this on my own without taking Worthy to get stitches.

"Where is the peroxide?"

I tore through the medicine cabinet talking to myself aloud.

"What else? What else? Antibiotic ointment."

I ran to the garage with my supplies to find Worthy laying on a pile of old dirty drop cloths. I approached him carefully and spoke to him softly.

"It's alright, buddy. What happened to you? I'm going to fix you up, okay?"

I stroked the top of his head. I didn't know if he understood my words, but I knew he understood my compassion. He knew I wasn't going to hurt him and I was there to help.

After several weeks of applying peroxide and ointment with the assistance of Worthy licking his wounds, the laceration had healed. He was no longer limping and seemed to be back to his normal self. I tried to rouse some applause from Nick, but my amateur vet skills were unimpressive to him.

"Worthy's gonna be okay. He seems to be healed up pretty well. I kept putting peroxide and ointment on him and he just has a pink scar now," I boasted like a child waiting for praise from a parent.

I was proud of myself for helping out my dog, but I was hiding disappointment I had in myself. Once again, I had folded under Nick's pressure and didn't take care of Worthy how he deserved. This was just a usual attempt to mask my weaknesses behind my abilities to be resourceful. I was hiding my lack of strength by appearing like I had things under control. My "can do" attitude would be a disguise for everything I couldn't do. This shouldn't be mistaken for turning lemons into lemonade. This was absolutely not the same thing. If I had no control over the situation, it might proved to be true. But I did have a choice and I chose the weaker path. I chose it out of fear. Nick was making threats and I believed he would see them through. If he shot a bullet into Worthy's skull, I genuinely believed the responsibility for his death would be on me.

"So, what do you think? I did good, huh?" I asked hopefully.

Nick's reply stung.

"I'm just glad you didn't make me shoot him."

CHAPTER 16

MARRIED – 11 YEARS

I dropped two arms full of paper grocery bags onto the kitchen floor. The kids shuffled in behind me flinging their backpacks and rushing to the pantry for a snack. The phone was ringing, my two oldest were arguing over the last pack of cheese crackers, and Carter was emptying out a kitchen cabinet. Blackness behind my eyelids calmed me briefly and I sucked in a deep breath. *Just breathe*, I told myself as I exhaled. *You can do this.*

Nick had been on a work trip for three days, and I was overwhelmed with stress. I got the kids settled down at the kitchen island with homework and hustled to get the frozen foods put away. The red blinking light on the cordless phone indicated, among other things, that it needed my attention. I pressed the play button on the machine and rushed around the kitchen tossing items in the pantry and refrigerator.

Nick's somber voice was muffled on the other end.

"Hey, it's me. I just wanted to tell you and the kids how much I love you. The plane is going down."

The message ended abruptly. My heart sank into the pit of my stomach as I listened to his words and replayed the message a second time. *Did I just hear what I think I heard?* I didn't want to alert the kids, so I did my best to maintain composure. *This could be it. This could be what I'd been wishing for all this time. Nick could be erased from my life forever.* My emotions were mixed as I watched my children playing together in the living room. They would grow up the rest of their lives without a father. *Would they miss him? Would they remember him?* Empathy generated feelings of sadness for them, but hate for their father made me not care. They would be better off without him and I wouldn't be to blame. As my imagination reenacted the horrific details of a plane spiraling toward the earth, my thoughts quickly switched to all of the other innocent people on the plane: mothers, fathers, friends, siblings and children. *God, I'm so selfish.* As I stared at the phone, my vision blurred from the tears I couldn't quell. I needed to call Barb.

"Calm down. I'll check flight statuses and call the airport. I'll call you right back. Just stay calm."

"He's dead, Barb," I cried.

"You don't know if that's true. You need to stay calm, dear. Let me make some calls."

I hung up the phone and said a prayer to God. I prayed Nick's plane wasn't rocketing straight to the ground. I prayed he would walk through the door with his computer bag like any normal day. *The plane is fine. All the people on the plane are fine. The pilots have control. Nick is going to come home.*

Phone clutched in both hands, I answered before the end of the first ring.

"Did you find out anything?!"

"I didn't find anything about any planes crashing. I'm not sure. I'll call again a little later. Just try not to get upset. I didn't see anything on the news either."

I was panicking. *How is she not panicking?* Her words didn't comfort me. My imagination mixed with my fears whipped around like a kite in a windstorm.

"This is like when those 9/11 victims got calls from their families after their planes were hijacked! What if that happened?! What if his plane was hijacked?! I tried calling his cell phone several times, but he never answered. What are we supposed to do?"

"You and I can't do anything right now. You just need to stay calm, keep the phone by you and wait."

She directed me with such serenity it was difficult to ascertain she was talking to me about her baby boy.

"Who was that, Mommy? Why are you sad?" Claire asked.

"Oh, it was just Meemaw. I'm fine honey," I said, wiping the wetness from under my eyes.

"Oh," she sighed with disappointment, "I was hoping it was Daddy!"

I forced a grin.

"Me too, honey, me too."

A few hours had passed and lots of concerned family members had called reassuring me everything had to be fine. But my body didn't believe them. The muscles in my arms and hands tensed to the point of shaking. My heart sank so low I could feel it thumping in my stomach. My armpits were wet with sweat, staining my gray fitted t-shirt. My mind was grasping for anything to hold onto as a good possible outcome.

Suddenly, the loud rumbling of the garage door interrupted my thoughts and Nick casually strolled into the house.

"What's wrong?" he asked.

The look of worry in my eyes quickly converted to rage. I was no longer concerned. I was furious. My brows crinkled and lips pursed as I tried to make sense of this emotional roller coaster.

"What?" He genuinely appeared confused.

"You said the plane was going down in your message! The whole family has been worried sick for hours!" I screamed.

The corners of his mouth slowly curved into an upward smile.

"It was a joke."

He cautiously bent over and placed his heavy bag on the hardwood floor keeping his eyes fixed on mine.

"A joke?! That's a sick joke!" I yelled at him.

"You never answer the phone, honey. You know it drives me crazy. I thought I would mess with you. You need to relax."

Before I could unleash more hostility, Claire came running towards him and tugged at his belt. I bottled my frustration and anger not wanting her to see us fight.

"Daddy, Daddy," she squealed, "hold me, hold me!"

He picked her up and wrapped his long arms around her tiny little body, and she nuzzled her face into his neck. I stood there firmly. I wanted an apology. I waited patiently as he focused all of his attention on Claire.

"Honey, get down and go finish your show, Daddy and I need to talk."

"Okay, Mommy," she said as she bounced off toward the couch.

A devious look encompassed his entire face. A sly smile and detached eyes unified his look.

"If you answered the phone when I called, this would have never happened."

"I can't always answer the phone! I have three kids to take care of and I don't have the phone glued to my ear."

"The ringer is set to six rings. It shouldn't be very difficult to answer it."

"You shouldn't have lied about the plane crashing!"

"Lower your voice. You know how much it bothers me when you don't answer yet you continue to do it. Do you even care about me? I can't understand why I have asked you so many times to just simply answer when I call, and you can't even do what I ask. It's like you're doing it on purpose to upset me."

The frustration inside me was scaling my insides and anxious to leap from my mouth. *How is this my fault? This is not fair. Does he really not think this is his fault?*

"I'm not doing it on purpose. I just can't always answer it!"

"I'm not going to talk to you anymore if you can't lower you voice. You won't answer the phone even though I've asked you nicely so many times before, and you still keep raising your voice when I am calm and respectful to you. You are not the partner and wife I was expecting when we got married. And now you're proving you're a bad wife."

I burst into tears as he walked away. He took no blame and, in fact, blamed me for the entire thing. There was no way of convincing him he made a mistake. He shifted the fault entirely to me, and I inwardly began to believe he was right. *Maybe I should answer the phone more. Maybe I should be more thoughtful about answering.*

"You should call your mom and let her know you're home!" I yelled.

Nick ignored me, unaffected by my emotions or any worry he caused anyone. There was no apology, no remorse and no empathy.

"Did you hear me?"

I followed him to the bedroom and approached him about calling his mom. He sat on the bed, opened a book and pretended I didn't exist.

"Nick! Why are you ignoring me?"

He was silent. This was my punishment for accusing him of wrongdoing. It would last several hours to several days, just long enough for me to absorb the guilt, take the blame and form a new behavior to help me avoid this in the future.

From then onward, when it came to answering the phone, I jumped. Avoiding an emotional event like this again would become a priority for me. The ill feelings I associated with not answering the phone could be easily avoided.

The phone would accompany me anywhere I went while I was home. Ringers would be set to high. I would check the phone multiple times per day just to be sure I hadn't missed any calls. I set the ringers for as many rings as possible before voicemail would pick up. If it rang once and I didn't have it on me, I ran as fast as I could to see who it was on the caller ID. If I had forgotten to bring the phone into the bathroom while I was showering, I'd stop mid lather and trail water and suds across the tile to reach the phone. The phone was Nick's instant connection to me. Making myself quickly and easily available to him was going to save me from a lot of grief. My behavior would once again adjust to his needs.

CHAPTER 17

MARRIED – 11.5 YEARS

I put my lips up to the plastic coffee lid and blew into the hole. The sweet scent of caramel macchiato floated up into my nostrils. I tipped the cup back and the hot liquid blanketed my tongue. Snow was falling outside of the tiny coffee shop where I sat nestled in a worn-out leather love seat. A young couple hustled inside the door, helping each other remove hats and gloves before heading to the counter. The grinding of coffee beans, gurgling of the brew and whistles and hums in the background were like a barista symphony. The coffee warmed my insides while the environment soothed my nerves.

It was short-lived. Sweet peace was interrupted by an unfamiliar and loud ring tone coming from my purse. When I pulled out my cell phone there was a notification. My GPS location was being pinged. Only one person had the ability to ping my location and it was my husband. I called him immediately.

"Why are you pinging my location?"

"Coffee, huh?"

"Seriously, Nick? I literally just bought it and sat down."

"I know. That's why I called. I get the notifications from the credit card company."

"I can get a coffee if I want to."

"Stop wasting my money on coffee. It smells bad and it's gonna make your teeth yellow. Do you really want to have yellow teeth and bad breath? I can't believe you continue to drink it after I told you how much it bothers me. You don't actually care about what I want. You need to stop."

I argued with him for a few minutes until I finally agreed to stop and go along with what he wanted. I left the coffee shop, but I lied to my husband. I lied to end the conversation. I lied because I couldn't bear the condescension and control. My plan was never to stop, but it was to lie and sneak it behind his back. The next time, I would use cash. Non-traceable cash.

Nick rarely caught on, except for a few times when I forgot to throw away an empty venti I'd left in the cup holder of my car. He would shoot an evil side-eye look of disapproval my way. It was a wordless threat. Silent sovereignty. It was intentional intimidation and I fell into the trap every time.

After years of hiding my coffee drinking and cash transactions, I decided to buy a coffeemaker. I claimed it wasn't for me, but for guests who would come to our house who might like to have some coffee. Keurig and single cup coffeemakers were becoming increasingly popular, but I bought a traditional coffee machine because it was cheaper and Nick most likely wouldn't notice.

Each day after Nick would leave for work, I would pull out my coffeemaker and brew a few cups of dark roast delight. Savoring it, and then buzzing around the house getting chores completed was routine. After each use, I washed and dried the coffee maker and put it away in the pantry where it was out of sight and out of Nick's mind. I did this every single time I used it, except the day I didn't.

I had just brewed a fresh pot of coffee when I got a text from my sister-in-law saying she needed me to watch her kids for an urgent matter. I rushed out of my house leaving my precious coffee, hot in the pot, on the kitchen counter. If Nick saw it, I had already rehearsed what I would say. The lie would roll easily off my tongue. I'd say it was the first time I used it and didn't even get a chance to drink any.

That afternoon, Nick came home from work early while I was gone. When I walked through the door, I saw him, but not my coffeemaker. My initial false optimism led me to the sink, thinking he may have cleaned it out for me. I was wrong. It wasn't there. *Where was it?* I didn't ask him about it, but I looked for it frantically for three days. I tore apart the house, the basement and even searched his car. *Had he donated it to Goodwill or had his mom store it somewhere?* I was frustrated and angry, but I refused to let him know.

On the fourth day I discovered the coffeemaker. It balanced unsteadily on a pile of random tools in the bottom of Nick's dusty, red, tool chest. I lifted it carefully from the tool chest and stored it in the kitchen where it belonged.

Excitement surged through me like a kid on Christmas morning. The rush I felt after finding it gave me such a sense of victory over him. This little stunt was not a game. It was my own husband flexing his muscles to do as he pleased. This was Nick exerting control over me.

He was sitting in the living room recliner using his laptop computer. I tiptoed quietly behind him and imagined what satisfaction it might give me to shatter the glass coffee carafe over his head. The pattern of his closely shaven hair bordered the perfect circle of his bald spot like a Jewish man's kippah. I studied his head, shook off the violent thoughts I was having about him and turned to start making dinner.

"I found my coffeemaker," I said, my voice unwavering.

"Oh, you found it?"

"Yes, and I'm not happy you hid it from me."

"Oh my gosh, will you lighten up? It was just a joke."

"A joke? You tell me not to drink coffee. You say you hate it, and you give me the third degree if you know I've bought it. It wasn't a joke. It was a punishment."

I caught my twisted facial expression in the reflection of the microwave glass. My downturned lips and squinted eyes highlighted my anger and frustration. Inner turmoil was increasing, and I was screaming inside.

"You are so sensitive. I can't believe you're getting this worked up about something this stupid. Why didn't you just ask me where it was?" he asked, patronizingly.

"I'm not sensitive. You are mean. You did it on purpose to be mean to me. Why do you have to lie about it?"

"Um. I don't lie. You are the one who lies. If you weren't sensitive, you wouldn't even be bringing it up. Obviously, it bothered you, but I was just messing around. You're just so angry all the time. I thought for sure you'd ask about it, and I would have told you where it was. It's sad you can't even take a joke and have a little fun."

Anger built inside me. He stayed calm. *How is he so eerily calm?*

"God, I can't believe you? You are such a liar!" My frustration lunged out of me like a rabid dog.

"Lower your voice, please. You are not acting like a good marriage partner right now. We should be able to have an adult conversation without you raising your voice. You're acting like a child. And you know better than anyone that I never lie."

My blood boiled. I felt the vibrations of rage beginning from my feet up throughout my entire body, ready to erupt from my mouth like dragon's breath.

"I don't have to lower my voice!" I yelled.

"I am not going to speak to you if you can't stop acting crazy. I didn't do anything wrong and you are overreacting. You need therapy."

He stood there, cold and unflinching, yet slightly amused.

"*I* need therapy!? Are you kidding me? We are married. *We* need therapy. Why do you hate me so much?!" I screamed. Resting my elbows on the cool granite countertop, I cradled my face in both palms. There was a long pause between us, and I waited for him to say something to disagree with my questioning accusation.

"Maybe you hate yourself for acting like this all the time? I'm not sure if you have PMS or something worse, but it's time to go to the doctor. Your mental health is suffering, and I think you need medication. You know I love you, but this is out of control."

My mental health? Maybe I am crazy. I'm not crazy. Am I? I certainly didn't feel normal. Something was wrong. Nick didn't want to see a marriage counselor with me. He had no reason to. The problems were inside of me.

The next morning, I dialed my gynecologist and listed all the things Nick told me about myself. The doctor followed my lead and wrote me a prescription for an anti-anxiety medication to mellow me out. He said it would take the edge off. It definitely did, but the problems in our marriage didn't fade. We were still arguing. I still felt horrible about myself and Nick was still complaining about me. I went to see many different therapists who let me cry on their couches and express my frustrations. But there was never a solution discovered by a therapist or even a medical doctor. Something was amiss.

CHAPTER 18

MARRIED – 12 YEARS

C reativity had always been one of my strengths. Math and sciences gave me struggles, and Nick made sure he was the only one to help our kids with those particular subjects. Art, music and anything creative were the areas where I shined. Nick knew this about me from the beginning of our relationship. Instead of encouraging my talents, he used them against me. Handmade gifts, fun surprises, and special days I set aside for someone I loved were my fortes. Not only did it make the receiver feel good, but it also made me feel good.

Years and holidays passed, but gifting to my husband became increasingly difficult for me. The joy in my gift giving quickly morphed into fear. It was no longer enjoyable to give him gifts. In fact, it gave me anxiety. I scoured Pinterest and Internet blogs for new and creative ways to surprise him. Everything had to be handmade, or I'd be chastised for buying presents requiring no thought, no effort and way too much money. It was unbearable to me to be at the receiving end of his condescension, so I avoided it at all costs, purely out of fear.

It was Nick's birthday, and the kids and I created a colorful poster board sign that read, "Best dad in the world lives here – HAPPY BIRTHDAY." At the bottom of the driveway by the street, I hammered the sign into the ground on a wooden stake I had found in the garage.

"Now, when Daddy comes home, he will see this first thing!"

The kids were so excited.

"Do you think he'll like it?" Lleyton asked, hopefully.

"Of course, he will! It's from you guys!"

The kids and I went back to the house, and I started up our beat-up golf cart we used to get around the property. With little hands trying their best to help, we filled it with a folding table and four chairs for the kids and Nick to have dinner outside. I would serve the meal. We loaded up the dinner plates, silverware, balloons and streamers and I drove the cart back to a large field behind our house. Claire helped me steady four large garden stakes as I hammered them into the ground blocking off a 12'x12' area with colorful streamers and balloons. We created a boundary as a "room" outside. We set up the table and chairs and placed a vase of wildflowers the kids picked for the centerpiece. A home-cooked favorite meal of meatloaf, mashed potatoes, salad, and green beans sat covered on the checkered tablecloth. Our three, little children and I met him in the driveway when his vehicle pulled in. They grabbed him by the hand and dragged him back to the field where his birthday surprise was set up. The kids each took a seat.

"Welcome to your birthday dinner."

He trudged over to the table slowly, talking with the kids and asking them questions about their day. I hadn't realized I'd been sliding a long strand of my hair through my fingers for some time when Nick alerted me.

"Do you ever stop twirling your hair," he asked with disdain. "That is so annoying when you do that."

I lowered my hand to my side to not agitate him further.

"The kids drew pictures for you and we made some poems about you," I smiled.

Nick took his seat and did the sign of the cross over himself to pray.

"In the name of the Father and the Son and the Holy Spirit."

The kids and I joined him in prayer. My palms were warm and moist. After the prayer, I rubbed the wetness off on my jeans

The kids and Nick ate and when they finished, I cleared the dirty plates and utensils. My hands slightly trembled as I lifted a heavy, glass pitcher. A simple compliment would have quelled my fears. Just a few genuine words of appreciation would have relieved me of the tension. Eager to hear his compliments of my efforts, I smiled and asked him if he liked his gift. My heart was hopeful, yet fearful as I waited for his response. His eyes went downcast to the table. His shoulders slumped over.

"Hey, I almost forgot!" Claire squealed happily and ran to the golf cart. She yanked out her clunky pink Disney CD player from the back of the cart and switched on some upbeat music.

"Daddy and Mommy have to dance now! Come on Dad, get up!"

Lleyton and Carter jumped up and ran off into the tall grasses flailing around and dancing erratically. Their arms and legs and little butts wiggling in no particular rhythm or pattern. A wide smile stretched across my mouth as I watched. Claire let out a howl of laughter as they ran circles through the field. I couldn't help but think of my sweet Worthy who would have normally been running around with the kids. He'd been missing for several weeks and, though I did everything I could to try to find him, sadly, he never returned. I thought about where he might be and why he ran away. I couldn't help but believe he got tired of the neglect and only hoped he found a caring human to love him how he deserved. Snapping out of my regretful reflection, I held out my hand to Nick.

"Well?"

"You know I don't dance. Don't make a scene in front of the kids."

"It would make her so happy."

Claire was fidgeting with the dials on her toy, intently focused.

"Dance with me, just for a minute."

"I said no. I never dance, and I'm not about to start now. This was your idea wasn't it?"

"Come on," I begged. "We're trying to do something nice for you. They're just kids."

He outstretched both of his hands in front of him as if he were tight gripping an invisible basketball.

"You are not listening! That is NOT what I asked you. This was your idea wasn't it?"

I nodded.

"It's really disappointing you don't consider me when you're planning for my birthday."

My optimism was short lived. I had failed. I walked over to Claire, took her hands and danced around the grass with her. Her giggles echoed through the field as I spun her around. Lleyton and Carter ran over to join in.

"Me next! My turn!"

My kids were so full of life and love and I immersed myself in their joy. I caught a glimpse of Nick at the table looking on at us, expressionless. The kids each got several turns of me spinning them around until I was too dizzy to keep going.

"All right guys; let's clean up and go inside now," I said as I let out a breathy sigh.

The kids ran toward the house. Nick rose up from his chair and followed.

"Well, happy birthday. I hope you liked it," I said.

"You always make me dinner, so it wasn't really any different than a normal day."

He shrugged his shoulders. I felt his hate and loathing of everything I did, deep in my soul. His face was blank as he stared at me waiting for my response. Those cold eyes rendered me still, as if they had some magical powers to paralyze me. The sun was blazing above us, and my children giggled as they ran after each other in the swaying grasses. The rapid chirps of the crickets in the distance matched my heart rate. I turned my gaze toward a murder of black crows perched on some dead treetops in the backdrop behind Nick. While his condescension loomed around me, I imagined the flock flapping down and pecking out his evil eyes as I stood by apathetically. An exasperated sigh escaped my lungs, and I swallowed hard to keep from crying. As I absorbed his disapproval, I felt my heart withering, weaker with each beat that once rushed love blood through my veins. Tears would be no match for Nick. I braced myself for his lecture and stood firmly, awaiting the emotional blows.

"You really think this was a good present?"

He folded his arms across his chest. His presence towered above me. Unknowing which response he wanted, I remained silent. Unsure of what to say or how to respond, I tightened my lips and flared my nostrils, hoping he would see my anger.

"Answer me," he demanded.

Engaging in an argument with Nick would only make me feel worse about myself. I never won. He never heard me. The problem with this continuous cycle was that the bar Nick set for me was totally unattainable. Each time I'd climb a little higher to reach the bar and Nick would move it up, just out of my reach. This happened repeatedly. *Would I ever be good enough? Could I ever really make him happy?* I wasn't sure. It definitely didn't seem like I would ever be what he wanted me to be. My faulty mindset of doing a little bit more and trying a little bit harder, kept me exactly where Nick wanted me to be, inferior to him.

"I'm sorry," I said, trying to show him all the sincerity I had inside me.

"I'm sorry too," he said. "Our marriage could be so much better if you actually cared about me."

Nick walked along the shortest part of the grass. He yelled for the kids to follow him, and I cleaned up the birthday mess I had made in the yard.

I was actually glad he walked away. His talks could go on for hours. The one-sided conversations were emotionally exhausting, circular and extremely confusing. I quickly learned the easiest way to end the chastising was to admit fault, even if it wasn't mine.

CHAPTER 19

MARRIED – 17 YEARS, THE MORNING AFTER THE NIGHTMARE

I got out of bed early to do some damage control from my nightmare and anxiety attack that interrupted Nick's precious sleep the night before. Breakfast in bed might be just the distraction and atonement I needed. I held out a plate of steaming scrambled eggs, bacon, and sliced, ripe tomatoes. Nick's laptop rested comfortably on his legs and his bare back was propped up by a heap of pillows at the sturdy mahogany headboard. My toes wiggled into the plush carpet beneath my bare feet as I waited for him to look up and take his food.

"I made you breakfast," I said cheerfully, hoping to draw the attention away from my episode the night before.

His head hung over the keyboard, and his eyes glanced up briefly at me as he let out a loud, sharp sigh.

"Can you just set it on the nightstand? You can see I am obviously doing something, right?"

"Well, yes, but I—"

"I know I've told you this before. It's like you don't even listen to me. It's extremely inconsiderate."

Rejection, hurt, and anger rumbled deep inside me and reflected to my nightmare, wishing it to be my reality. Anger welled up from somewhere deep inside me and exploded from my mouth.

"You are such a jerk!" I yelled, slamming the plate on the nightstand.

"I deliver you breakfast in bed and you treat me like this?"

"You need to lower your voice," he whispered. "I'm not yelling at you so please don't yell at me."

"How am I supposed to act when I do something nice for you, and you can't even take the damn plate?!"

"You're supposed to act like a normal person and not cuss at me. You're not acting maturely right now."

"Stop treating me like I'm your child! You are not my father. You're my husband."

It took everything I had in me not to pick up the plate and dump it on his head. I imagined a pile of eggs slopped over his balding head with thick chunks dripping onto his skinny bare shoulders.

"Stop acting like a child, and I won't need to treat you like one."

Every ounce of self-control in me was garnered so I wouldn't explode on him. He was so calm and so matter of fact, and all I wanted to do was scream.

"You need help. I really think you need to be medicated. Normal people don't wake up in an emotional breakdown for no reason like you did last night. Just look how you're acting right now. You need to call a therapist or a doctor and get this fixed today. Something isn't right with you."

"You mean a nightmare? People have nightmares, Nick."

"That was more than a nightmare. Something's wrong with you. Something's seriously wrong. You need to be prescribed something. I don't know what, but something for sure."

He was right. Something was very wrong. I felt like a shadow of myself. I wasn't who I used to be before I met him. Therapists and doctors gave me their input, but no one seemed to truly be able to help me. Outwardly, I appeared to be a normal and completely productive part of society. *"You seem fine to me." "This is perfectly normal." "You are just stressed, try taking some time for yourself." "Take a little vacation."* They all said the same things.

Professionals couldn't pinpoint the problem. I couldn't pinpoint it either. I didn't have extreme stresses, like a death of a loved one, an ill child, or loss of a job. Something didn't add up. Nick always said he knew what was wrong with me, though.

"You're crazy and we both know it. You need to control your emotions. You are just mean. You snap at me and the kids." The lecture began. I braced myself. *Don't cry.*

"What I don't understand about you, is why you are always in a bad mood when you have such a perfect life. What do you have to be upset about? Do you know how lucky you are to have the life you have? You get to stay home and be with the kids all day while I go to work. I would give anything to be able have your job, but I can't because I have to support you and pay for everything you buy."

"Pay for everything? Are you serious? You *control* everything I buy." The words jumped off of my tongue to defend myself from the attack.

"You didn't let me finish what I was saying. Quit interrupting me. Something is seriously wrong with you!

Something is wrong with your brain. I'm really concerned about your mental health."

He peered at me under his unruly brows, studying my face like I was some sort of alien. As he waited for me to respond, hot tears welled in my eyes. My mouth was gaping to defend myself, but no words would come out. He shut his computer carefully.

"I still love you, honey, even though you're crazy. I'll never stop loving you." His tone changed. His demeanor was softer, calming. Unaware he was patronizing me; I still ate up his words like a hungry wolf.

"Look, you can fix this because I know how smart you are. But first, you have to admit it. You *are* crazy."

The knot forming at the back of my throat was swelling. I swallowed repeatedly to prevent myself from crying. My husband injected his lies into my brain like venom, dissolving my thoughts and paralyzing me internally. Confusion swirled throughout my veins like a mystical sedative, disorienting me. I believed I was fortunate to be loved by him, despite the mental instability he accused me of.

As I stood there, by the bedside staring at Nick, I internalized the guilt for all of our marital problems. Outwardly, it appeared he wanted to help me, but I never seemed to be able to help myself. His calm demeanor and apparent concern for me felt genuine. Nick was normal and I was broken. My craziness was spilling over into our marriage and if it failed, there would be no one to blame except me.

"Look up the number on my employer's website for free phone counseling and talk to someone today."

At this point, I was willing to do whatever Nick told me to do. I'd gone to therapy alone many times before. Whenever we had issues, I went to therapy. Nick awaited the full report from each session because I needed help. He was driving our marital ship and I continued to follow his orders so we wouldn't sink.

When I reached a telephone therapist, I regurgitated the words Nick used earlier. He stitched those ugly phrases all over my body like a surgeon with no anesthetic. His needle punctured and pained my flesh as he sewed the lies deep into my skin trying to pierce my soul.

"I don't know what's wrong with me. I'm just overly emotional and I'm too sensitive. I lash out at my husband and my kids. I am downright mean sometimes. I have mood swings and I'm feisty and irritable all the time. I have anxiety attacks, too. I don't want to be like this. I'm constantly in a bad mood and I don't have any reason to be. I'm really lucky, but I feel so much anxiety and stress, and I just want to curl up in a ball and shut out the world." My voice cracked as I tried to hold back tears explaining how broken I was.

"Are you under any unusual stress?" She asked.

"I mean, not anything unusual. I have three children and I've stayed home with them since they were born. They fight and argue sometimes. I do all of the housework and maintain the yard and the garden because my husband works. So, yeah, I guess it causes me some stress, but this doesn't feel normal to me. Something is wrong."

It sounded pathetic when I verbalized it. Complaining made me hate myself. I felt guilty for acting like a whining child with first world problems. But in my gut, I knew something wasn't right. *Something isn't right.*

The only thing I knew how to do was take all the responsibility for the problems in our marriage. Assigning blame to Nick was pointless. He never accepted any responsibility, even when I pointed out his flaws. This became glaringly evident after several failed attempts to coax an apology from him. It never happened. By absorbing the fault, I was giving myself a sense of false control. A mindset like this gave me the bogus feeling I could fix it. If I was the problem, then it was I who could make it right.

Claire, Lleyton and Carter came barreling through the door with my mother-in-law right behind them. She placed a plastic grocery bag on the kitchen island and smiled at me.

I quickly wrapped up the conversation with the therapist. She left me with some names of marriage counselors Nick and I could visit. After hanging up, I felt hopeful. Nick and I had never been to marriage therapy together because he said he didn't need it. I'd been several times alone, but this lady had suggested we go together, so I was hopeful he might attend this time.

The kids were playing and giggling and the joyful sound of their squeals and laughter sent warmth through my body.

"Mommy!" They screamed. "We missed you!"

They flung their little arms around my neck as I kneeled to greet them, and we all tumbled to the carpet. The shared joy among the four of us lifted my spirits. Snuggling up with my sweet babies was the closest thing to heaven I could imagine.

"I missed you, too," I laughed.

Tangled up with them on the living room floor, I lay there thinking how blessed I was to have these three, healthy, amazing kids. The sun shined on us through the giant living room window, warming my face. I had a beautiful house surrounded by nature, wonderful kids and a husband who I believed truly loved me. It didn't seem like I really had anything to be upset about. It seemed I was broken, and my husband was immaculate. *Maybe being a wife and mother isn't what I was built for. Maybe I do have a mental disorder.* There wasn't an answer. There never had been. I didn't know what it was, but I knew something had to be done.

"Everything okay?" Barbara asked.

"Yeah. Everything's fine. Nick and I are going to talk to a therapist because we just keep arguing all the time."

"Oh," she said solemnly. "I guess a little marriage counseling can't hurt anybody. You know you can always talk to Father Beiting at church. He's always willing to help with marriage issues."

Barbara reached into the grocery bag and pulled out a brand-new dish scrubber and dish-drying mat. She held them up, one in each hand for me to see.

"These are for you to replace your old ones."

"There's nothing wrong with mine."

Barbara laughed, picked up my sink scrubber and dish mat and gently dropped them both in the kitchen garbage can.

"Those are awful, and you need new ones."

"I like my scrubber!" I shouted.

She shook her head at me.

"You crazy girl. These are both better than what you were using before."

Nick walked casually into the kitchen and greeted his mother with a hug and a kiss on the forehead.

"Thanks for watching the kids," he said.

"I got the name of some marriage counselors to meet with, and this lady said your work will pay for three of our visits. Just give me a couple of dates and times you are available, and I'll call to set up the appointments."

My optimism beamed as I fully expected him to be thrilled I had explicitly followed his orders. I waited, anxiously for him to respond. But within minutes of hearing my statement, Nick went on full defense mode.

"I'm not going to see a therapist," he said, "you're the one who needs therapy, not me."

The back of my throat burned again as I held back my urge to scream at him again.

"Kids, go put your sleeping bags away, and then you can go outside and play."

I paused, breathed in slowly and exhaled. *Stay calm, Allie.*

"You won't even go with me? To support me?" My voice quivered with the question.

"I don't need to go to support you. I already support you. I think you need to go and fix whatever is wrong with you."

I felt alone and defeated. This pattern ensued over and over during our marriage. Fights erupted and Nick convinced me I needed help. I sought help, and Nick sat back and waited for me to get better. Not once did he ever attend a therapy session or doctor's visit with me regarding the crazy he accused me of.

"Come on. What could one session hurt?" Barbara asked.

"I'm not going. I don't need therapy. She does."

"Why won't you go with me? I feel like you don't care about me."

My eyes welled up with tears. Upon seeing this, Barbara exited the kitchen and went back to the bedroom to help the kids and removed herself from our awkward confrontation. I'd wished she stayed. She was my only hope of convincing him to go.

"You don't feel like I don't care about you. You feel badly because you treat me badly. You know I care about you. You just don't care about our relationship and it shows when you try to put this on me, saying I don't care about you, which I clearly do."

What? What kind of word puzzle is this? What is he talking about? My head hurt trying to understand him. Nick was so skilled at inciting confusion in me. I felt stupid and intellectually inferior. And then I felt angry.

"What? I don't even understand what you're talking about. You can't tell me how I feel. You aren't me."

"I know you better than anybody. In fact, I know you better than you know yourself. So, don't try to tell me I don't know how you feel, because I do. I always have."

Parts of me were disappearing right before my eyes, and I felt helpless to stop it.

"But I *feel* like you don't care when you refuse to see a therapist with me. You're my husband and we are having problems. I think you need to be there."

Begging him made me feel powerless. Pleading for support for our marriage felt wrong.

"Listen honey, I don't need to be there when you are the one with the problem. You're the one with the emotional issues. You're the one who is oversensitive and erratic, not me. This is a *you* problem, not an *us* problem. I know you better than you know yourself. I believe you want to get better. I know you want to be a good wife and mother. You're just not doing a good job of it. Maybe you need to be on medicine. Maybe you just need to talk to a professional. I don't know what the solution is, honey, but you have to do this on your own. I've tried to help you, but you don't listen to me. You need to get a hold of this."

"But I—"

"Stop interrupting me when I'm talking! It's incredibly rude," he snapped.

"Stop treating me like one of your employees! You're not my boss!"

He was silent and glaring at me. I'd gone too far. *Fuck, he's mad now.* I lowered my voice and apologized.

"I'm sorry for interrupting you, but I thought you were finished talking."

"No, you didn't. You call me names, now you're lying to me. You really disappoint me, you know. You knew I wasn't finished, and you interrupted me because you thought of something you wanted to say. I wish you would just listen sometimes. That's part of your problem, too. You don't listen. And then you lie about it."

He continued to drone on like a slow freight train and I zoned out. Lectures like this were normal and the escape route for me was to simply tune him out. It saved me from having to hear about how horrible I was, but it negatively impacted me because I never could recall what he said. It infuriated him.

Nick walked over to me and he pulled my chin up with his hands. I looked away.

"Look at me. I love you. I'll never stop loving you. You may be crazy, but I'll never leave you. You'll always be my little, crazy Allie."

He smiled sweetly, patted the top of my head and gently brushed a tear from under my eye. He wrapped me in a big hug, tight to his chest.

He tried to comfort me, but it stung. I felt small and weak. I felt sad and angry. I also felt very, very crazy. With my face pressed into his chest, I considered what he said. *Am I crazy?* I inhaled the scent of the clean detergent from his shirt. *I am always the one messing things up.* I felt his heart drumming softly through his chest. *I am always upsetting him. I really love him. I try so hard, but I can't seem to do anything right. I need to try harder. I don't feel normal. I feel like something is wrong, but I don't know what it is. God, help me.*

CHAPTER 20

MARRIED – 17 YEARS

It was a typical Sunday dinner at my in-law's house, something we did religiously from the beginning of our relationship. Each of my husband's older brothers, their wives and all of the children were in a tight, little circle with his parents. This was a place where outsiders were unwelcomed. It was a sacred family day set aside for only this family. Everyone attended church, and shortly afterwards, went to Mike and Barbara's house for a day of food and family. The women prepared and cooked the meals and the men sat in comfy recliners, drank beers, and watched television. The kids slammed doors as they ran in and out of the house, playing and enjoying time with their cousins.

After everyone finished eating, the women cleaned up the food and dishes and swept and wiped down counters, while the men went back to their seats to relax. This was how it was for the entire time I was in this family.

One particular Sunday, Nick, our kids, and I had arrived before any other family members. Barbara was outside basting food on the grill, and Mike was in the garage, scrubbing a small grease stain off his immaculate concrete floor. The kids ran to the swing set, and Nick and I entered the house and sat down on his parent's plaid sofa. The windows were open, allowing a strong breeze to waft in the smell of barbecued chicken throughout the house. Nick and I were not in love anymore. We lived like roommates in the same house. Sadness weighed heavily on my heart every day and I didn't know how to be happy anymore. I had been hinting to him how unhappy I was, and I sensed Nick knew. He wasn't dumb. My behaviors were changing. My attitude was callous. I argued more and listened less.

"We need to go see a therapist." I said.

Nick shot me a side-glance of disapproval.

"I'm serious. We don't get along. There's no love in our marriage. We need to go."

He finally had enough of my suggestions to involve a professional to help repair our marriage. He knew neither of us was happy in this marriage. All of the negativity involved between us was pinpointed on me. I felt trapped, like a prisoner, silenced and worthless. The only thing I knew how to do was involve a professional. If you're sick, you go see a doctor. If your marriage is in dire straits, you go see a marriage counselor.

"If you want to go see one, go see one. I won't stop you. In fact, I think you need to, and I will support you 100 percent."

He was curt and callous. Again, shoving all responsibility in a two-way relationship onto me. Naturally,

I was livid. He indirectly insinuated I should absorb all the blame for our marital problems. *How dare he suggest only I need to go?*

In anger I yelled out, "This is OUR marriage, and it's not going to get fixed by only one of us going to therapy."

"Listen, if you want a divorce, I'll fully support you."

I was completely taken aback. This was the first time he ever said the word 'divorce' to me in reference to our marriage. *He's bluffing.* He was trying to make me believe he didn't need me. My widened eyes were locked on his cold expressionless face.

"But hear this, if you divorce me, I'll do everything in my power to take the kids from you and I will get full custody of them."

"You can't do that! No judge will ever agree to that!"

He was severely underestimating my intelligence. I knew he was bluffing, and I knew he was lying. The audacity of his statement was ridiculous, yet infuriating.

"We'll see," he smirked, shrugging his shoulders in an attempt to solidify his front. I rolled my eyes and stormed outside to tattle on him to his mother.

"You won't believe what your son just said to me!"

I replayed the conversation to her, word for word and she listened intently as always. The thick chunks of meat sizzled as she flipped them with her tongs. I waited anxiously for her to give me some sort of reinforcements for how I was feeling. She took a deep breath and exhaled the statement like she'd been holding it in for an eternity.

"Well, he definitely could take them from you."

"What?! No judge would ever agree to that. On what grounds?"

Her declaration put me on the defense immediately. I sensed my walls building up like virtual bricks on a fast forward time lapse. There was nothing I could think of where a judge would yank my children from me and place them in the arms of their father. It made absolutely no sense. I searched the files of my mind for something, anything. She interrupted my frenzy with a lie.

"Your drinking."

I was immediately shocked. Barbara never drank alcohol and she looked down on those who did. My drinking consisted of weekend social drinks with family, friends, and, of course, Nick. Both he and I were casual drinkers and it wasn't unusual for us to have a beer or occasional glass of wine at a party or family gathering.

"My drinking?! What do you mean? That's not even true."

Barbara carefully tended to the chicken on the grill, babying and turning legs and breasts gently with her tongs. She waved a plume of smoke from her face.

"He'd have family witnesses."

Instantly, I felt my heart beating in my stomach. Barbara had just removed her true mask in front of me. She blatantly tossed away the blindfolds of justice I had always seen her wear. But, surprising to myself, I wasn't mad at her for it. I was mad at myself for believing she could love me as equally as her own son.

It seemed everything she did was to preserve the façade of her perfect, little family. *Were her intentions true? Did she really want to help so much? Was there another motive behind her help? Why did she spend so much time catering to her adult sons and their needs, especially when they were fully capable of doing things for themselves? Why did this pristine, outer image matter so much to her? What was she hiding?* And that's when I figured it out. She was hiding the brokenness she had created. She was concealing the evil she had raised. She wanted the world to think she had succeeded when she had failed. It was a complete lie. And then, after all those years of being married to her son, she was so very fearful I'd shatter the false images she created by disrupting her pristine apple cart.

It was clear Nick was never going to attend a therapy session with me. I didn't know what else to do. I was sandwiched between two brick walls. I took out a legal pad of paper and wrote down three, full pages front and back of every single reason Nick hated me. It included my actions, my inactions and basic things about my personality. As the ink spilled onto the pages my heart ached. I had never in my life felt so unloved. Maybe, if I wrote down the things he hated, I could start one by one and fix them. It seemed daunting as I looked at the pages sprawled out before me. *Maybe this would help. Maybe a therapist could read through this and advise me.* I was fully defeated and completely tormented. *My life would be so much easier if Nick would just die.*

CHAPTER 21

Following my morning routine as I woke, I unlocked my phone and pressed the little white bird icon with the blue background. Habitually, I thought I'd be scrolling mindlessly through Twitter to find something to engage in, but I was wrong. Notifications were blowing up my phone. I rubbed my eyes and peered closer to see what was happening. My frustration rose when the app locked up due to the influx of notifications. As soon as I'd swipe one away, another would appear. Quickly, I went to my settings and shut off the notifications to figure out what was going on. One little reply I had made before falling asleep the night before had created quite the stir while I slept.

Instantly, I was filled with excitement. Pride welled up within me. People were approving of me. They liked me. They really liked me. I felt like Sally Field at the 1985 Oscars. For someone with eroded self-worth, this was just the boost I needed. They thought I was smart and witty. The affirmations were the little seeds I needed to begin my personal transformation. The connection with other adults assured me that I wasn't alone. Being isolated from the rest of the world was torturous and social interaction revitalized me. It was necessary for me to function. It was needed for my survival. The heavy stones of self-doubt I'd been lugging around started to disintegrate with each follower I gained. There was a huge discrepancy between what Nick made me believe about myself and what the Twitter community was revealing. As a person with very low self-worth, I almost didn't buy into it. Doubt and belief played tug of war, but Nick's dubious words over the years were like Hannibal Lector on steroids.

The positive feedback and supportive interactions were so uplifting. I was accustomed to criticism at home and my husband refused to have conversations with me about real world news and politics. But the strangers in my phone didn't refuse and Nick was taking a backseat to Twitter. Not only had it become a source of joy for me, but it was also a place of solitude where I could get away from him. I could immerse myself in all the wonderful feelings I'd been lacking for years. The people on Twitter were like-minded to me and we shared similar beliefs and morals. I felt happy and safe in my little world of Twitter. My opinions were wanted. I felt smart and funny and good about myself. These were all things I yearned for from Nick and things he was purposefully withholding. I couldn't understand it.

Throughout my interactions with others, I had made several new friends. I was developing relationships with people online and there was one person, in particular, I gravitated to. His name was Johnny. He was intelligent, funny, fiery, and bold. He assisted me with learning to navigate the Twitter forum and understanding some of the pitfalls in relation to Internet trolls and bots. His knowledge of technology was extremely helpful and it directly contributed to the surge in my popularity online. Behind a little horseshoe avatar was a great friend to me in the cyber world whose wisdom and opinions I valued immensely.

"Wow, do you really need to get on Twitter the minute you wake up?" Nick huffed as he noticed me tapping away on my phone with replies.

Shut the fuck up, asshole.

"Leave me alone, Nick."

"You've really changed and I don't like it," he stated.

"Okay." I shrugged my shoulders, uncaring and uninterested.

"You're not the person I married. You're so aggressive all the time. It's like you want to fight constantly. Not just with me, but with everyone. I asked my mom about it and she agrees. You instigate arguments with my brothers, their wives, everyone. I don't get it. I think you're acting like this because of Twitter. You should think about how it's affecting you and our marriage and stop using it. It's making you a different person."

An immediate sense of rage overcame me. He was trying to take away my solitude, my freedom, my joy and my friends. A tingling sensation crawled up my legs toward my stomach and ultimately to my face and burst out of my mouth. *I wished he would just die.*

"No!"

"No?" he asked, surprised by my defiance.

"You're not going to tell me I can't be on Twitter. Maybe I have changed. But I don't think the change you are referring to is a bad thing."

I held my phone tightly; worried he might try and take it. I threw the blanket off of me, tossed it onto Nick, and stormed from the bedroom to the hallway to get away from him. Goosebumps rose up like a tiny army across my bare legs. I went straight to the digital thermostat to see it was set at 68 degrees. I pressed the arrow up a few times for more heat.

"What are you doing?"

I jumped, shocked at how stealthily Nick had approached me from behind.

"It's freezing in here. I'm turning up the heat."

"No, you're not. Here you go again. Doing whatever you want with no regard for anyone else. I pay for the heat in this house. Sometimes I think you just do this to cause arguments."

He aggressively hit the down arrow with his long index finger setting the heat back to 68. His arm blocked my way and I ducked underneath it to move away from him and walked into the living room.

"I'm not picking fights. I'm just standing up for what I think. I don't have to sit back and accept what other people say. I can say whatever I want!"

My tone rose in a distinct inflection as I defended myself.

"Lower your voice," Nick whispered, slowly. "Can you hear how I'm talking to you? Can you hear how I'm not raising my voice?"

My eyes rolled so hard in my sockets I could feel the muscles contract in pain.

"You are so unbelievably rude. And why do you think it's okay for you to roll your eyes and yell at me? Maybe you need to get your hearing checked."

"I can hear you just fine! And I don't have to lower my voice!" I deliberately yelled louder.

"Please calm down. All I'm saying is you've changed. I have been the same person I have always been since you met me. I am consistent and you are the most inconsistent person I've ever met. I repeat in case you didn't hear me the first time: I'm the same as I've always been and you are the one who's changing."

Immediately, I knew why he hated the changes in me. I was standing up to him. My defiance was a threat to his control. I was becoming independent in my thoughts and actions. I was becoming a threat to his hold on me. However, I had already decided I liked who I was becoming and I was not going to go back to where I used to be. The fire inside me that he had snuffed to an ember so long ago was about to be reignited.

Every day, and multiple times a day following, Nick would comment on my Twitter use. He watched my usage through his own newly created Twitter account. He deliberately and obviously kept his eyes on my phone and me. When I discovered those accounts and blocked him, he had his friends and family spy and report back to him so he could confront me.

Though I had made it very clear I wasn't going to stop using it, he was still trying to convince me otherwise. He would comment that he didn't like the posts I had written. He told me my tweets were inappropriate and too bold. He said I was neglecting my chores around the house and I wasn't spending enough time with him. The fight in him was strong, but I was not willing to give in. I think Nick began to realize I was no longer dependent on him. For the first time ever, I was putting myself first.

His strategy was to regain control over me by eliminating my independence. It meant removing access to the rest of the world. *What was he shielding me from? What didn't he want me to know? What was so important that I didn't find out?*

"You're not the person I married and I want that person back," Nick played this part pitifully. His pathetic demeanor was paired with a childlike whine.

"People change, Nick. You're right. I'm not the same person I used to be, but there's nothing wrong with that. I'm changing for the better. I'm stronger now."

Nick disagreed. He knew I was slipping from his grip. He pointed straight at my face and stared down his finger like it was the barrel of a gun.

"You need to get off your phone and make breakfast for the family."

"You make breakfast! You know how to pour a bowl of cereal!" As soon as the statement left my mouth, I felt power surge through me. Nick disappeared out of the living room back towards our bedroom and all I kept wondering was, *'Why couldn't he just disappear from my life forever?'* More than ever, I wanted him dead.

"Great partner you are, Allie!" he yelled sarcastically down the hallway before slamming the door behind him.

I plopped onto our plush couch and pulled a throw blanket over my bare legs. A message notification from Johnny caught my attention.

Johnny: *Hey, How are you?*

I responded quickly and proceeded to text him the details of the morning about my and Nick's argument. He listened carefully and expressed his sympathy for what I was going through. He didn't immediately offer any advice, he just heard me out like any good friend would. It felt better to vent, especially to someone who wasn't in my inner circle. Nick had taken away my confidence, tightened a blindfold over my eyes and kept me within the confinements of his family.

As the days passed, I found increasing comfort in Johnny and my admiration for him grew. He became a sounding board for my personal, marital issues. Johnny was the only person I felt I could vent to. He was always available for me to ask questions of and get a male perspective. Over time, I had shared specific situations about what I was going through with Nick. Johnny was aware of the stress and frustrations I was experiencing in my marriage. He was fair and unbiased when listening and I valued his input and cherished our friendship. He gave me confidence to stand up to Nick.

Johnny: *Allie, I think you need to know something. I don't want to overstep my bounds here, but I really care about you and I'm worried you don't know what's going on in your marriage.*

Allie: *What do you mean 'what's going on in my marriage'? My husband's a jerk.*

Johnny: *I just need to be totally honest with you about this. The things you have told me about are very concerning. I have lived in a lot of places and I have experienced a lot of different people in my life. Your husband has some serious issues you should be looking at based on the things you have shared about him and how he treats you.*

Allie: *What do you mean?*

Johnny: *Ok, don't freak out when I say this but I know what a psychopath is when I see one. I have experienced people like this in my life and I'm certain Nick is one.*

Allie: *A psychopath???!!! LOL*

Johnny: *I'm very serious. I'm not joking about this. Listen, psychopath or sociopath, whichever term you prefer, the label isn't as important as you knowing what it is. I know you probably think of the Hollywood version of a psychopath. This is NOT the dramatized version of what the movies makes everyone think. This is NOT like the movies. This is NOT theatrics. I'd strongly suggest you read up on what sociopaths, true psychopaths and narcissists are. I am confident this is what you've been dealing with your entire marriage. But first, do yourself a favor, turn off your Wi-Fi when you search it and erase your browsing history afterwards. One thing you do not want is for a sociopath to know you are onto them. You can never tell him he's a sociopath, a psychopath or even a narcissist. His abuse tactics will change, making it even harder for you to navigate the confusion.*

Allie: *Are you serious???*

Johnny: *I'm very serious. I don't just throw out things like this for no reason. I can answer questions you have about it, but just look into it. That's all I'm suggesting.*

Allie: *Ok, I will.*

Most of my thoughts about this were draped in doubt. *Could this really be the reason for so much of the angst in my life? Could my husband, whom I've loved and lived with for so long, be someone I never knew he was? Could I be in an abusive relationship? Was I being deliberately mistreated and manipulated by the one person who is supposed to love me?* These questions were bouncing through my mind like invasive tumbleweeds in an Arizona desert.

Disbelief, skepticism, and despair, to name a few feelings, haunted me daily after Johnny revealed this. Even though he exposed this information, my heart still wasn't sure.

I didn't look into it immediately like I told Johnny I would. There was no way on earth I was dumb enough to marry someone like that. I was a good judge of character.

Still, I wasn't happy and I wanted to be stronger. So, over time, I began standing up to my husband to test my strength. Oftentimes, I'd look for opportunities to disagree with him. Even if I agreed with him, I would argue just to argue, playing the Devil's advocate unbeknownst to him. I know this infuriated him, but it helped me to grow. I never won the arguments. I never won anything with Nick. But the thrill of a heated discussion with him where I felt like a fighter was beginning to change something inside me. Time and again, I'd get theoretically knocked down and put back in my place. Nick looked down his long nose at me, proud of himself for beating me once again. David and Goliath before the battle, it seemed we were.

I would glare at him as he reveled in his superiority while I sat defeated and plotting my next attack. *But how was I going to beat him?* The answer was in change; the exact change Nick accused me of was my only way out. I had to continue changing, or I would be permanently positioned in a dark place of fear and anxiety. The latter was no longer an option for the rest of my life.

Ultimately, something needed to be done. Though I desperately wished Nick would just die and disappear from my life, I knew the likelihood was low. My fantasies and dreams of his death vanished like candlelit flames in the wind. No matter how hard I prayed and wished for his demise, reality consistently let me down. I couldn't kill my husband. I was going to have to leave him.

CHAPTER 22

MARRIED – 17 YEARS, 2 MONTHS

My dad knew something was wrong by the urgency of my request to meet him for lunch. We had a booth at the back of the restaurant. He took a sip of beer from the bottle and I stirred my ice water with the straw, watching it swirl and clink in the glass.

"What's wrong, sweetheart? You seemed so upset on the phone. I'm worried."

Killing my husband to rid my life of the constant anxiety and stresses I had wasn't an option. The only real solution was for me to divorce him. Speaking the "D" word out loud was frightening, but actually following through with a divorce would be like having to saw off my arm to save my life. It would be the most difficult and most painful thing I'd ever do. But I had to do it. If I stayed, I would suffer the death and loss of my soul. I had already lost so many other parts of me to Nick and I refused to let him take everything. I was fully aware that, when I finally walked away, I wouldn't be unscathed. The pain and suffering accompanying the divorce would just be something I'd have to endure.

"Dad, I don't want to be married to Nick anymore."

The Harley-Davidson logo on his faded t-shirt blurred as my eyes filled with tears. He rested his strong forearms on the table and clasped his leathery hands together.

"Aw honey," he sighed, "did something happen?"

"Yeah, Dad, something's been happening for a long time."

I reached into my purse and pulled out a thick folded wad of yellow papers. He took it from my hand and carefully unfolded the three pieces and flattened them out on the table between us.

"What is all this?" he asked, peering at the papers and smoothing the wrinkles and creases.

"This is why I want to leave, Dad. I wrote down everything he hates about me. I don't want to be married to someone who can't stand me."

He reached into his pocket and handed me a clean handkerchief.

"Thank you," I muttered.

"You wrote all this?"

"Yeah. A few days ago. I didn't know what else to do. It feels like he hates me and everything I do. I thought maybe, if I wrote down all the things he hates about me, it could help me to improve."

A gray-haired woman walked over to drop off a basket of bread and take our orders.

"You two cupcakes know whatcha wanna eat yet? Just got some real good fried green tomaters, just delivered from the farmer's market."

I turned my face away from her, pretending to look at the dessert menu on the wall. Dad told her we needed a few more minutes to decide.

"Take your time, hon. Holler when ya'll are ready."

He leaned forward and studied the notes I had scribbled on the papers. I watched as his eyes darted and scanned the list of all of the things Nick controlled in my life. His brows furrowed and he shook his head in disapproval.

"I'm so sorry. This is a lot. Have you talked to him about this?"

"No, Dad, I just don't think I can do it anymore. I try so hard, I really do. But this has been going on for years and I'm exhausted. I don't have anymore energy in me to keep trying. I don't know what to do. I think divorce is the only way."

He rubbed his trimmed, peppery beard, contemplating what to say to me, his eyes locked on the inked words. They poisoned my soul. I was yearning for some words of wisdom from him. My need for clarity and direction was immense. He was the only person I had told my secret to and I didn't have plans to reveal it to anyone else.

"You know, when your mother and I divorced, it was the worst experience of my life. It was the hardest thing I ever went through and I don't wish that on any of my children. Being separated from you and your mom was excruciatingly painful for me and I loved your mother very much. Divorce is not something I would suggest. You should talk to him about it and try to work on this with him. You have your kids to think about, too. I just want to see you happy and I'm sure you two can work this out."

It wasn't what I was wanting or expecting to hear. It wasn't the rescue I needed. Ultimately, I trusted my dad and I went to him because I knew he would have a perspective I didn't. He had been through divorce. He'd experience the struggles and heartaches associated with such a difficult life event. Before speaking with him, I had assumed he would have gone along the same path as me, pushing me in the direction I was already headed. After all, I was hurting and at a crossroads.

"Well," I hesitated, "maybe you're right. I don't know. Something just doesn't feel right. I have been sad for so long. I feel trapped and frustrated and confused."

"You never told me about this. Why?"

He slowly twisted his wedding band clockwise around his finger. Was he thinking of his first marriage to my mother or his second marriage, to my stepmom?

"I don't know. I didn't want you to be disappointed. I felt like a failure. I thought I could fix it. I tried so many things but I can't make him happy. I feel like I'm at the end of my rope. I am just totally exhausted. I really wanted Nick and I to be married forever. That was the plan, you know? Like Grandma and Grandpa," I sniffled and wiped my nose.

"I know. I hate seeing you upset like this."

"I've fantasized about getting in the van with the kids and just driving to Mexico and never coming back."

Telling him about my fantasies to kill my husband wasn't necessary. My dad knowing things were bad enough for me to kidnap my own children would be alarming enough.

He awkwardly scooted the breadbasket towards me; I took out a brown roll, played with it, and nervously picked at it, piling tiny pieces on my plate.

"So, what should I do?"

"I can't tell you what you need to do. This is your life. But I can tell you I regret not trying harder and I really don't want you to have to say the same about your marriage someday."

Prior to my conversation with my dad, I was ready to begin the process of leaving Nick. Maybe I really was just hoping he would see the hurt and sadness in my face and tell me get the hell out of my marriage. He didn't tell me to go, but he didn't tell me to stay. I believed my Dad had my best interests at heart, but one thing was for sure, he had never been on the receiving end of the type of treatment I endured and I needed someone else to guide my ship. There was no way for him to fully comprehend the level of angst I was feeling. In all fairness to him, I hid most of it from him on purpose, pretending my marriage was just about perfect.

"I just don't know what to do."

There was an overwhelming turmoil within me. Weight was coming off from my lack of appetite. Physical illness plagued me frequently. Anxiety attacks, weight loss, double vision, eye twitches, and nausea were common and worrisome to me. Memory loss and confusion became a standard for my brain. Something was wrong and, though I'd always believed it was me, I was beginning to think it wasn't.

"It's going to be okay, sweetheart. Just talk to him about this and try your best to work it out. If I could go back in time, I would have tried so much harder to work things out with your mom. For me, for her, and for you."

The tear-soaked handkerchief was wadded in my hand.

"I'll wash this and give it back to you later."

He waved it off.

"Keep it."

"Thanks, Dad. I mean thanks for the advice."

"Everything is going to be fine," he assured me, "but call me if you need anything."

On the drive home from meeting with my dad, I decided I was going to make one last-ditch effort to rescue my marriage. Throwing away all those years was painful to think about. Something inside me was still conflicted. My dad's advice and the sadness I felt from his experience took over my instincts. I'd been suffering for so long in this poor excuse of a marriage, but it didn't matter. Red flags would be ignored again. I would push aside what my gut was telling me to do, go against my instincts just as I did when we married, and continue to try harder once again.

CHAPTER 23

MARRIED – 17 YEARS, 2 MONTHS

I pulled into the disheveled garage and shut off the engine to my old, dented minivan. So many thoughts were going through my mind, but I knew I had to focus on the one and most important thing—saving my marriage. Walking away now and throwing away all of my adult life with this man seemed crazy. We had healthy children, a beautiful home, and some bumps in our relationship. My internal voices were arguing with each other, the logical one disgruntled at my innate ability to downplay reality.

Finally, I made up my mind and messaged Johnny. If I was going to repair the brokenness in my life, I had to make some decisions to put my husband and my marriage first.

Johnny and I had developed a very caring and positive friendship. I had no doubts he would understand my decision. Still, I felt at a loss even thinking of cutting off my friend. But I knew it was something I had to do in order to keep trying to save my marriage.

Allie: *Hey*

Johnny: *Hey. What's up?*

Allie: *I need to talk to you about something.*

Johnny: *Sure. Are you okay?*

Allie: *Sort of. Idk. I had lunch with my dad today and long story short. You know how many issues Nick and I have been having? Well, I decided I need to focus on our marriage. I need to try harder to save it. I'm going to delete my Twitter account.*

Johnny: *Oh.*

Allie: *I decided I need to stop communicating with you and spending so much time on here so I can really focus on putting my marriage first. I'm really sorry but I'm going to get off of Twitter and shut it down. I don't think I should be communicating with anyone here anymore.*

There was a long delay before I received a response. Tears were streaming down my face as I thought about losing my friend and my solace. Johnny was there for me in so many ways: A trustworthy friend, a supporter, an encourager, and a teacher. I felt like I was about to toss a precious gem into the depths of the ocean.

Johnny: *Allie, that's fine. I understand. However, I want you to know you're making a huge mistake. No. Not because you're choosing him over me. Because you're choosing him, over YOURSELF, again. It doesn't matter if it's me or Twitter or anyone else. But* *you're choosing a psychopathic and sociopathic relationship over who you truly are. I've mentioned several times in great detail how and what a psychopath and sociopath is. I've seen who you truly are. And this evil coven isn't it. Good luck.*

To end the conversation, I replied with only a sad crying face emoji and closed the messenger. *Have I done the right thing? Is this a mistake? Surely my husband isn't a psychopath. He's never even said a cuss word to me! Surely Nick isn't a sociopath. He's not crazy and rarely even raises his voice.*

Had I stumbled upon the true root of my problem or was I looking for a convenient excuse to leave an unhappy marriage? This possible epiphany was suspended between what I thought I knew about Nick and *what* I feared he might be. Ultimately, I didn't want to believe he was capable of such evil, so, temporarily, I didn't fully accept it.

Something inside me still wasn't settled. This didn't feel quite right. I pulled out my phone, turned off the Wi-Fi, and began a Google search like Johnny had instructed. I typed in the word "PSYCHOPATH." As I scrolled the page, I noticed an article titled, *"The 20 Traits of a Psychopath."* What I read shocked and astounded me. The more I read, the more I realized how right Johnny was. This was Nick. The traits described him almost perfectly. Each link led me to different articles, and I mentally earmarked insight and verbiage I had never heard before. I was unrestrained as I took screenshots of pages and scanned articles to reference.

"Superficial charm, grandiose sense of self, cunning and manipulative, lack of remorse, superficial emotional responsiveness, lack of empathy…" and the list went on mirroring things I knew about my husband. My eyes

widened as I digested this awful revelation and I felt the inside of my head spinning in disbelief of my new discovery. A sick feeling overcame me, and my entire body was quivering. I'd been living with a real-life monster for my entire adult life.

I could no longer view Nick the same way. His secret was exposed and I was the one person he didn't want to know it. I knew what he was up to now. I knew he was a liar and a con artist. He was a selfish demon hiding behind the mask of Christianity. He put on a disguise of being a good husband and a good father—a disguise I was no longer fooled by. I would not take my eyes off of him going forward. Anything he did or said from then on would be scrutinized under a microscope. I obsessed over Internet research and library reading material from then on out. I took notes and jotted revelations in my phone's notepad. Finally, I discovered I could be free of him and I had every intention of being just that.

Allie: *Johnny, I'm so sorry!*

Johnny: *What?*

Allie: *The Psychopath stuff! You were right. I had no idea. I'm sorry I didn't believe you. I just started reading about it and now I'm really scared. He's never hurt me before and I don't think he will. I just don't know what to do now.*

Johnny: *People don't like the word psychopath because it sounds like a serial killer! That's Hollywood stuff, not real life, like I told you before! These are psychological personality disorders. I've experienced several of these types of people very intimately in my* *life, even growing up. Psychopath, sociopath, narcissistic personality disorder, call it whatever you want, they are all EVIL. And just because someone doesn't physically hurt you or never has, doesn't mean they aren't destroying you emotionally and mentally. You didn't seem to want to know the truth, no matter what I said to you before. I just figured it was your life and you needed to work it out.*

Tears were flowing uncontrollably now.

I screamed out in anger, "How could he do this to me?! Why would he do this to me?!"

Unfamiliar and intense emotions burned my heart like a welder with a blowtorch. The pain was profound and I pressed both hands over my chest. My eyes darted around the room irrationally looking for some sort of indication as to why Nick would do this to me. The stark contrast of *"Nick would never do this to me"* and *"I am going to kill him"* swapped back and forth in my mind. Trying to distinguish my anguish from my rage kept me on the edge of insanity. I didn't want to believe the truth, but I was finally finished ignoring my instincts. What I had just discovered would be the knowledge that would save me.

Allie: *I just feel so stupid!*

Johnny: *Keep reading and keep educating yourself. I'll help you in any way I can if you have questions. But you're onto it now. You are not to blame. You are not stupid and this isn't your fault. Do NOT forget it.*

Allie: *Thank you! I'm so sorry I didn't understand before. I'm sorry I doubted you.*

Johnny: *It's ok. I'm just glad you finally see so you can protect yourself. The great news is you are finally enlightened. The blame is lifted from your shoulders. The burden of being the reason for every single problem goes away now.*

Allie: *The things I've been reading advise not to give any emotion around a sociopath. They say to act "gray" and to avoid engaging with them.*

Johnny: *That's right. You are a drug to him. Think of yourself as heroin. Him, as the addict. He will do whatever it takes to get the next hit, the next feeling of euphoria. Your emotion is the drug. Your reaction to his abuse is the drug too. Have you ever seen what happens to a heroin addict when their supply is cut off? They lie, cheat, steal, manipulate - just to get what they need. More drugs. Nick is no different. Psychopaths are no different. Eventually, he will get tired of trying so hard to get what he wants and he will move on to easier targets. So be gray like you said. This is your best protection against him. It will do you no good to tell him or anyone else, including a therapist about what you think. It actually could harm you because his strategies will change and pull the rug right out from under you.*

Afterwards, I spent weeks researching. I watched videos and read blogs and psychiatric articles on mental health disorders. I was diagnosing my husband and he wasn't even aware of it. Now, fully aware of what I was up against, I was determined to use every resource possible to defeat him.

CHAPTER 24

MARRIED – 17 YEARS, 3 MONTHS

I woke with a pounding headache and a feeling that I might lose whatever contents were still in my stomach from the night before. I rolled over and pulled the thick comforter over my head and buried my face into my pillow.

"How are you feeling?" Nick asked dryly.

"Mmmmm." I groaned in reply, trying to avoid his typical father-like lecture.

"We need to talk about your behavior last night."

My heart rate spiked, and it felt like a 3-inch nail was being hammered into my skull.

Not now, I already feel like shit. Can't this wait 'til later? Maybe if I just ignore him, he will go away. Maybe he would leave me alone. Who was I kidding? Nick loved to lecture. It was his favorite thing to do.

"I'm serious. I'm your husband and I'd appreciate it if you'd show me some respect. We need to talk," his tone sharpened, and I cringed.

I braced myself for the haughty judgment I was about to endure. *Here it comes. God, I just want to go back to sleep. Apologize, Allie. Get it over with.*

"I'm sorry. I know I drank too much. I don't need a lecture."

The words mumbled from my lips like an old tired car engine, pushed past its lifespan. I rolled over to face him and tucked the blanket under my chin. I hoped he'd believe my apology and just let it go.

"Yeah, you did drink too much. You embarrassed yourself and embarrassed me. Adam and Jenny don't want to hang out with us anymore because you can't control yourself."

"Did they say that? I don't believe you! Jenny's my best friend. Adam's your brother! You were encouraging me anyway! You like it when I drink. And you say I'm more fun when I drink. The one time I have one too many, you chastise me but don't say a word about it while I'm drinking?!"

My voice progressively rose in volume as if it were racing to meet my anger build up.

"Can you please lower your voice?" his volume lowered to a whisper. "I'm not your dad. You should know when to stop drinking."

I rolled my eyes, hard, purposefully attempting to over-exaggerate the absurdity of his comment.

"That's funny, Nick, because you say you're not my dad, yet you act like it all the time, constantly telling me what to do."

"Do you want a separation?"

"No! Of course not," I lied, "that's ridiculous."

I looked away. I so badly wanted to be truthful. I wanted to hurt him like he had hurt me. But I was too afraid. Somewhere deep inside me was a wisp of courage I couldn't extract. I knew it was there, but it wasn't enough to help me right now. I also knew I didn't love Nick anymore. I wanted out of this lame excuse for a marriage and, solely out of fear, I'd been dreaming he would just die.

"Are you sure? Because last night after we left their house, you told me you wanted a separation." I felt the blood rush to my cheeks, flushing them crimson. *Fuck...did I say that? Think Allie, think. You were so drunk. He kept encouraging you to drink.*

"I don't remember much about last night. I certainly don't remember saying THAT."

I disregarded his comment. There was very little memory left over from the night before and threatening Nick in any manner was just something I never did, alcohol or not.

"Well, do you? Because you *did* say it. Do you want to be separated, Allie?"

He continued to prod at me. *Why is he pushing me so hard on this?* My heart rate jumped, pulsing even harder in my wine soaked brain. The pain worsened. I paused. Not knowing how to proceed or what to say, I went with my go-to suggestion for our marriage.

"I think we should probably go talk to a therapist." I said nervously.

"Seriously? This again? Why? Do you want to divorce me?"

"No!" I lied again.

"Then what is it? Why do we need to see a therapist?"

"I don't know. I guess I'm just not happy. I think we need to talk to someone professional."

"You *guess* you're not happy? What could you possibly not be happy about? You stay home every day while I go to work and do whatever it is you do around here. Real rough life you have."

Sarcasm seethed from his lips like a pestered snake.

"Listen, honey, I've told you many times before, if you're not happy, YOU go talk to whoever you want. I don't need to talk to anyone. If you're unhappy, that's on you."

Annoyed and frustrated, with a pounding head, I pulled myself out of the bed and gingerly walked to the shower trying to keep my heart rate steady. My stomach churned. These conversations never went anywhere. He would dismiss my feelings and blame me once again. I was backed into a wall as usual. I was wrong and he was right. I lose again. This was nothing new. The tiny wisp of courage was still there. *Use it Allie. You have to use it now.* I yelled to him from the bathroom.

"I'm scheduling an appointment with a marriage counselor this week. This is OUR marriage, not MINE, and if we're going to fix it, then I'm not going alone."

"Fix what," he yelled back, "I don't understand what is even broken!"

"I told you. I'm not happy."

The acoustics of my words on the tile shower walls reverberated in my ears.

He had to know I wasn't happy. He didn't seem happy either. *Did he ever listen? Did he ever believe me? Did he think I was joking?* I told him over and over again he was chipping away at me and, one day, there would be nothing left.

I turned on the shower and stepped onto the wet tile. The hot water beat on my neck and back while a thick steam rose all around me. I shut my eyes. *I hate you.* Thinking of him just made me more upset. So, I went somewhere else in my mind, somewhere without Nick. Somewhere Nick couldn't find me. Somewhere he never existed at all. It was my comfort zone, on a sunny beach, all alone, except for a few seagulls gliding in the wind, and no

Nick. I lathered my hair and inhaled the scent of generic vanilla shampoo. The suds flowed down the drain and I imagined they were all my worries disappearing. I turned around to reach for the conditioner bottle.

In my peripheral vision I caught a figure standing by the shower door and a stab of panic rushed through me. My body jerked but I caught my balance before slipping on the suds below.

"Nick! Seriously?!" I screamed. "How many times have I asked you to please stop scaring me?!"

His scruffy unshaven chin rested on the edge of the smooth tile wall. He laughed with delight as the juvenile in a grown man's body startled my peaceful escape. He stood there staring at me, eerily waiting for my reaction.

"You know how much joy it brings me," he laughed. "Why do you want to take joy away from me?"

"It doesn't bring me joy at all. In fact, it scares the crap outta me and I hate it! So please stop it!"

"But it's so funny! I can't quit doing it," he smiled and batted his eyes as if he were a small child. "Just so you know, I'm not going to stop." His face quickly changed to stone cold seriousness.

I breathed a heavy sigh of helplessness and slumped my shoulders. Nick perched himself on the edge of the garden tub until I was finished.

I shut off the water, grabbed a plush white towel and dried off in front of him. He paid no attention to my naked body. Glancing at myself in the mirror, I noticed my hip bones were beginning to show. My body was withering.

"I want to talk about this some more," he said.

"Well, I don't want to talk about it anymore."

As I entered the walk-in-closet to grab my robe, Nick came in behind me and quickly shut the door. His tall frame was blocking any hope of me exiting on my own.

"Please move."

"No."

"I said move!"

"No."

I reached for the doorknob and he grabbed my wrist.

"We're going to talk about this, right now."

"Let go of my arm!" I yelled. "I want to get dressed."

His strong grip and long fingers squeezed tighter.

"I'd like to go get dressed now. Move out of my way!"

He stood like an oak tree. I attempted to push him with my body and pull the door open but my slight muscle was no match for his strength. He laughed at me like a big bully on a playground. Nick finally released his grip, but the invisible ropes he tightened around my wrists were still there. Any time I pulled too far from his control, I could feel the burn of woven fibers twisting against my flesh. Invisible yes, imagined no. The shackles he had on me were very real. He was so careful in public not to reveal his true identity. He could turn it on and off like a light switch, smiling and laughing with strangers, family, and friends and instantly turning to a monster upon the latch of our door.

I knew the discussion was unavoidable. The only way out was to give in to his demand. I was trapped and I'd already spilled the truth in a drunken state the night before. I hated tequila and even the smell of it would induce my gag reflex. I don't know why I kept topping off my glass, but I enjoyed the numbing as it happened. I threw my hands in the air.

"Okay, what, Nick?! What do you want me to say?!"

"You tell me. You're the one who wants a separation."

He crossed his arms tightly across his chest and leaned back against the door.

"Look," I snapped, "I just think you don't like me anymore. You pick apart everything I do. Nothing I do satisfies you and you never seem happy with me. If you aren't telling me with your words, you're telling me with your facial expressions. You know what? I think if you put together a job description of what you expect out of a wife and mother of your children, no one in their right mind would want that. You would be all alone without me because nobody would ever do what I do for you. No one. You would miss me for the things I do for you, but you wouldn't miss me for who I am. I just don't understand why you hate me so much? I annoy you daily, nothing I do is ever good enough and we never get along. It just doesn't make any sense. Why would you want to stay married to someone who you hate?"

"I don't hate you, I love you."

But Nick's actions toward me didn't match his words. How could he love me and treat me like this simultaneously? I felt like he was mind fucking me. Everyday I yearned for his love and acceptance, but I never felt it.

"Do you love me, though? I don't know. It doesn't feel like it. What I do know is I've been so worried about making you happy that I forgot I deserve to be happy too."

Nick was quiet. I was scared. Like sheet lightning in the distance with no audible thunder, I watched him and worried when the storm would crack. I waited for him to erupt. He said nothing.

"I feel like I do everything for you and all you do is complain about how I can't do anything right. You don't seem to appreciate what I do around here, and you rarely do anything for me. I'm tired. I'm just really exhausted from trying so hard to make you happy and it never works. I think you would be happier without me because, with me, you don't seem happy at all. I don't feel liked and I definitely don't feel loved. I'm trying my best, but I'm spent. I don't know how much more I can give. I think we need to talk to a professional about this. I don't think it can wait if we are going to try to fix our marriage."

I'd given Nick so much of me. I was starving while he sat fat and happy. I was withering away for him, an anorexic for love. He gorged himself on my spirit, feasting like a king. Something had to be done and Nick knew I was serious. For the first time I could recall, he was lost for words. I had spit out a summary of my feelings in a few short sentences hitting him hard.

I was stuck in a vicious cycle. Nick took what I had to offer him and tossed it away like garbage. I came back with more the next time only to watch it be discarded as well. I felt broken, defeated and lifeless. *What was so wrong with me? Why couldn't I make him happy? Why wasn't I good enough for him? What else could I do to be better so we could be happy like we were when we first met?*

Each time, I would try harder and harder to make him happy. He would raise the bar, and I would jump higher trying to grasp it. Chasing illusions was my job. My energy was depleted. Exhaustion overwhelmed me. Each day, I was approaching the finish line of a marriage marathon as my husband moved back the ribbon mile upon mile.

CHAPTER 25

MARRIED – 17 YEARS, 4 MONTHS

"The therapist appointment is this Friday at one o'clock. We need to be there a few minutes early for some intake paperwork. I'll text you the address."

I was finished with politely requesting and begging Nick to go to therapy with me. This time, I told him. His skinny shoulders were slumped and his neck hung, barely strong enough to hold up his pale, unshaven face. The faint purple bruising under his eyes outlined his bony sockets. Outwardly, Nick's appearance revealed his inner despair. Like a junkie coming down from his last high, the desperation was eating him alive. After drunkenly blurting I wanted a separation, I think Nick took me seriously for once in our life together. I was changing.

He locked a longing gaze on me as I sat at my computer, pretending to be busy.

"Do you need something?" I snapped, avoiding eye contact.

He shook his head and spun to leave the room.

I wanted to be as far away from him as possible. The sight of him sickened me. The thought of him disgusted me. Nick was walking around our home like a victim. His manipulation game was strong, but I was finally onto him.

Later, Nick and I settled into our normal nightly routine. We sat down for family dinner, put the kids to bed and then he and I watched TV in our bedroom with no words between us. To avoid a confrontation, I brought cheese and grapes in for my snack since Nick demanded crunchy foods not be eaten while he was watching television. I remained silent while his basketball game was on, as I wasn't permitted to talk during sports.

Shortly after the TV was off, Nick curled up onto his side and wept. I can recall only one other time I had ever seen him cry and it was after his grandfather's funeral. I knew Nick's fear of me leaving had nothing to do with true emotions. He knew when I walked away, I was taking the cleaning lady, the cook, the gardener, the driver, the Administrative Assistant, the caregiver, the servant, and half of everything we owned. Everything Nick constructed was going to be ripped from his grip by me.

Anyone would be upset to relinquish all of those things. Losing his wife wasn't the problem. But losing his position of authority and self-imposed superiority would be a devastating hit.

As my husband lay there next to me in a defeated heap, he said no words, just sobbed and heaved between his cries. His face was shoved into his bed pillow. The muffled weeping surprisingly amused me. The most Oscar worthy of all was his admission of fault. I knew it and he knew it too. Nick reached a point of desperation he'd never known.

"I screwed up everything. How could I be so stupid? I ruined everything," he moaned.

His over-exaggerated emotional breakdown paired with taking the blame for our failed marriage was like nothing I had ever witnessed. This man never exposed his emotions and never once took the blame. I had to admit, this was good stuff. I loved it. I was grinning inside. It made my heart swell. For a brief time, I felt like a bad person, but I swiped it away like an annoying phone notification. I knew Nick's act was pure narcissistic magic. Basic trickery, Acting 101. Simply put, it was one final effort to get me to believe him so he could retrieve his false power back.

While lying in the dark, I closed my eyes and channeled my inner actress to fake comforting a grown man who didn't deserve an ounce of sympathy. *Two can play at this game*, I thought. I gently stroked his back. The thin undershirt was damp with sweat on my fingertips as I ran my hand gently up and down his spine.

"Everything is going to be just fine."

I said it aloud for him to hear. The reassurance was for me though, not for him. It wasn't going to be fine for Nick, not in any way.

His rib cage expanded and contracted with each breath and his body quivered with his performance. *Wow, he is good.* His manipulation wasn't going to work this time. I was dead inside. I was impervious to his cries. A sly smile crept over my lips while he wept. *So, this is how it feels to win?*

"Everything's gonna be fine. It's all gonna be just fine."

The next morning, I woke to my alarm at six o'clock, as usual. I woke the kids and ordered them to be quiet as we all tiptoed around the house not to wake their dad. Nick liked to sleep in, so I always got up with our children. I made breakfast, helped them dress in their uniforms, and made sure they brushed their teeth and hair. I ensured they weren't forgetting anything, loaded everyone in the van, and drove to their private, Catholic school. After I dropped them off, I came home and made Nick's breakfast and lunch just in time for him to leave for work.

"Can you *please* not put an apple in my lunch bag?" He peered into the soft-sided cooler. "I've told you this so many times before. I get free apples at work." The shrill in his voice stretched for my ears. I winced.

"And can you stop making me things for breakfast I can't eat in the car? How am I supposed to eat pancakes in the car?" He huffed, irritated by my incompetence. I couldn't help but notice how quickly his attitude had changed from last night. It didn't take but a few seconds of disapproval for me to fall right back into his trap. Almost instinctively, I fell prey to his poison. I felt myself snap back into a position of weakness.

"I'm sorry." I nervously picked at the skin around my nails, not realizing I'd pulled off a little too much. Blood rose to the surface.

"I thought you could eat the pancakes before you left for work."

"No, I can't. I don't have time now! You'll have to give me some notice if it's something I can't just grab and go."

Nick hurried out the door and the feeling of inferiority and shame encompassed me. The rejected pancakes were still steaming as I slid them into the garbage. I stared at them, feeling sorry for them, lying atop a pile of other unwanted trash. They were flat, lifeless, useless and wasted; totally unwanted and unappreciated, just like me.

CHAPTER 26

MARRIED – 17 YEARS, 5 MONTHS

The days and hours leading up to our therapy session, Nick looked awful. He wasn't sleeping or eating. He looked like a novice tightrope walker, gently stepping one foot in front of the other, peeking at the ground below and fearing the fall. Sweat beaded on his forehead, lungs filled desperately with air in fear it might be his last breath. I had never seen him afraid like this.

He glided slowly into the home office where I sat staring at the computer. He sailed in so gently and quietly he seemed to float like a ghost.

"I am working from home today," Nick chose his words carefully, "so we can ride together to see the therapist."

I had already decided I was going to drive myself. Being trapped in a car with him for any length of time was excruciating. I had nowhere to go. This was his favorite place to lecture and manipulate me. There was no escape in a moving vehicle. My options were either engage in conversation or refuse to talk to him. Of course, jumping from the car had run through my thoughts many times but I never had the courage.

"We'll be driving separately. I don't want to be in the car with you on the way there and back from our first therapy session." I said bluntly.

His eyes widened and his face paled.

"Is it going to be that bad?"

He was fishing for information. He hated the unknown and feeling of powerlessness. There was a secret locked deep in my soul and he didn't know what it was. I think he had a clue, but I was going to force him to sweat it out until we met with the marriage therapist to hear it from me.

"We can talk about it with the therapist." I said.

Standing my ground was indescribably difficult. I had no practice in standing up to him. On the outside, I did my best to project an image of strength, but inside there was a petrified little girl.

He hung his head and trudged from the room like a scorned child.

I was scared. I was more scared than I showed to him and I was more scared than I'd ever been in my entire life. Leaving a dysfunctional relationship with a person who has abused you emotionally is like waking up from a coma. All of a sudden you have to figure out how to do the most simplistic things in life again, like saying 'no.' You have to re-learn how to be yourself. During the course of our toxic relationship, I felt myself being gradually erased. My involvement for this lengthy amount of time with Nick caused me to do everything I could to please him. Avoiding conflict was paramount. My continuous efforts to prevent arguments and constantly thinking about what Nick wanted felt like I was on a thin sheet of glass. The feeling of walking through minefields kept me in a continuous state of anxiety.

Nick trained me this way. He conditioned me slowly over time to behave just how he wanted. Nick didn't have to tell me to be home in two hours. Every time I went somewhere, at the one and a half hour mark of being gone, he'd start calling, texting, and pinging my phone using GPS. I was careful with my words and my actions. Less than commendable traits began to surface from within me for self-preservation; lying, sneaking and faking, to name a few.

Nick preyed on my weaknesses and used them to attack me. Before meeting him, I always thought of myself as being a good person, a kind and generous significant other and a faithful Christian. But when he saw any type of slip up from me, he used that opportunity to tear me down with the exact things I was most proud of. Often I said to Nick, *"You just keep chipping away at me. Don't you realize eventually there will be nothing left of me?"*

He always scoffed in reply or told me I was being too sensitive. *"Lighten up, take a joke, be mature"* were a handful of his go-to phrases.

He'd say he was just as hard on me as he was on himself. He claimed his overly high expectations were not reserved only for me, but for family, friends, co-workers, and even acquaintances. Over time, I began to believe I was overreacting and I needed thicker skin and should toughen up. Whatever lies he had told me about myself, I eventually believed. Meanwhile, I tried my best to not slip up, so I could avoid the negative feelings associated with not meeting his expectations.

All my adult life was spent with Nick. I really didn't know much else beyond the walls of my home with him, his parents, and siblings. As a little girl, I had dreamed of meeting a good man, getting married, having kids, and living happily ever after. I knew I deserved love and I would make a great wife. Then, when I met him, I thought he was everything anyone could ask for. He was intelligent, caring, funny, positive, religious, successful, charming, and kind. But all those things were gone within a matter of months as the glaring evil was exposed in him within the privacy of our home. Once I was in it for the long haul, and he knew I wasn't going to leave, he changed. My dreams were shattered and the lovely, little life I had envisioned was ripped right out of my heart, tossed on the ground and set aflame.

He was a monster hiding behind a smile, pretending to love me with words with no meaning or action behind them. I was conned. I fell right into his trap and everything went according to his plan, until I realized what I was dealing with.

My husband was not just a controlling man with some annoyances and irritations toward me. He wasn't just a typical jerk husband. He was a master of manipulation, a contemptible con artist and a champion of deception. I continuously felt like he hated me and anything I did was wrong and not acceptable to him.

I believe Nick hated himself but presented a false ego to give others a perception of confidence. For him to be happy, he had to shine the spotlight on areas of my life, my habits and my behaviors to keep the focus off of him. He did this exceptionally well because I began to believe he was better than me in almost every aspect of humanity. I felt I was a failure and fell short consistently. In the rare instance Nick paid me a compliment or showed me kindness, I felt a surge of hope. He dangled these sparkling jewels of reassurance to keep me hanging onto him. He showed me a potential that never really existed. The glimmers of hope had me holding out longer for the dream he originally sold to me. A dream that would never come to fruition.

Nick already knew how unhappy I was. I'd been eluding and outright telling him these things for years. It really didn't matter anymore. I was already checked out of the marriage and I had already made up my mind. None of the chipping away, or the manipulation and control mattered anymore. As soon as I walked into the office of the therapist, I was going to free myself from his cage. My mind was made up. This was my one chance to take it. Only I had the power to do so and it would be the moment Nick would free fall into despair.

For the first time in years, I didn't feel defeated. I felt like I held power. Make no mistake, I was very uneasy. I didn't know how to handle this newfound control over myself. I was surprised and unaccustomed to holding all the cards in what seemed like a stacked deck. I was the only one who knew what was to come during our therapy session. This was going to be excruciation for Nick and me both.

I stared at the wall clock in Dr. Lavalle's office, convinced the minute hand never moved. I fidgeted with my hands and silently prayed for strength to get through the next hour. I had been sick to my stomach for weeks leading up to this. My appetite was low, and my anxiety was high. At home, I tiptoed around Nick and avoided him at every opportunity, so sitting right beside him and waiting on the therapist was agonizing.

I knew something about him no one else knew, not even Nick. He had never been professionally diagnosed, but I knew exactly what he was and I had been discovering new and terrifying things about him. He was able to mask to the general public things only I was exposed to. There were so many things he hid outwardly but let me see freely. It was like living with two different people. The one in public was very different from the one behind the closed doors of our home.

Prior to meeting with Dr. Lavalle, I had researched extensively about how to deal with someone like Nick. I suppressed my emotions around him. Nick was gaining something from me that fed him like a drug addict: my empathy. Nick couldn't feel emotions like other people and was able to elicit reactions from me to satisfy his hunger for feeling. Feeling anything. It was a very difficult task for me to suppress my natural emotions. My nature is vibrant and emotional, feisty and excited. It was my personality. It's who I was. Nick said it was the first thing that attracted him to me. Now I understand why.

I looked at my watch. *How much longer do we have to wait?* The doctor was already fifteen minutes behind. I breathed out the air I didn't realize I had been holding in my lungs.

"Are you okay?" Nick asked carefully.

"Uh, yeah. I'm okay. I'm just frustrated the doctor is taking so long."

"Well, hopefully it means she's good." Nick tried to lighten the mood.

The heavy door opened and out stepped a young couple and a thin woman with long, wispy blonde hair streaked with gray. She walked up to us and shook both our hands and looked us over behind her small, circular framed glasses.

"I'm Dr. Lavalle. Come on in to my office and make yourselves comfortable." She pointed at two chairs, one for each of us.

My solar plexus swelled between my ribs. My armpits were moist. I crossed my arms tightly across my chest. I focused on the doctor and rehearsed in my head the things I had been practicing telling her. *I've been very gray with him lately. I'm not happy in our marriage because of how he treats me. He is very controlling. He manipulates and chastises me. I feel degraded and unloved. He startles me frequently when I ask him not to. He doesn't respect my wishes or wants. I think he hates me.*

"So, tell me, Allie. Why did you want to come here today?" she asked.

She jotted down a few notes on her notepad and crossed her hands on top of each other in her lap. She tilted her head and her warm compassionate eyes locked with mine.

I could see Nick staring through me out of my peripheral vision. I looked straight ahead at the therapist. My back stiffened as I prepared to unleash the truth I'd been holding inside for so long.

"I don't want to be married to him anymore and I need help exiting the marriage."

The words spewed from my mouth like dragon fire. I'd been holding them back for so long and the relief of it was like submerging my whole self into a warm, still bathtub. My secret was now exposed. The divorce monster I'd been hiding in my womb was now screaming, naked and vulnerable in the delivery room of Dr. LaValle's office. Nick knew I no longer wanted to be his wife. And, most impactful, he knew I rejected him as my husband.

I heard a faint whimper. I looked over at him and he was clutching his chest as if I had just stabbed a dull kitchen knife into his heart. *Another show.* I was unaffected. I didn't even try to comfort him. *Thank God for the separation between our two chairs.*

The doctor began asking him questions in response to my news. I looked at him. I heard sounds coming from both of their mouths, but I wasn't hearing actual words. Giving in was not an option at this point, but my self-confidence was still shaky. Falling for his lies and manipulation right now would be the flat lining of my soul. I knew I had to be strong and I knew I could not continue like this any longer.

My memory of what occurred in the therapy session was murky. I used the one and only therapy visit Nick ever attended with me to deliver the news to my husband that I wanted to leave him. It was a safe place for me since Nick might have trouble using circular logic and manipulation to keep me in line. It was there I knew his anger or frustration wouldn't be turned into a sales pitch as to why I was wrong and why he was right. I had to do it this way because, when you deal with someone like Nick, you don't win. You lose. Except when you leave.

"Why didn't you just tell him to fuck off?" she asked me, leaning forward in her chair and popping a stick of gum into her mouth.

Did she just say what I think she said? I was completely shocked. I contemplated her question as I watched her squish the gum between her molars.

"A piece?" she asked, holding out the pack towards me.

I shook my head.

Fuck off, Nick.

I imagined what it might feel like to say those words out loud to him.

Fuck off, you asshole.

It had never occurred to me I could say those words to him.

Fucking fuck off, you Mother Fucker!

"Well? Why didn't you?"

Dr. Lavalle waited patiently for me to respond, casually squishing the wad between her teeth.

In all the years of knowing Nick, I'd never heard him say one curse word. He expected the same from me and telling him to "fuck off" never entered my mind as a possibility to combat the control he imposed on me.

Verbalizing those two little words would be an invitation for Nick to further psychologically abuse me. Standing up to him would entice him to emotionally tear me down. A lecture, then a silent treatment would weaken me further while evil glares and gossip behind my back with his mother would be my final consequence.

"I was afraid," I admitted.

I was so scared to leave him. I was afraid of what he might do and how he would react. I was afraid he would use his manipulation and control to convince me to stay. I had to be realistic, his control over me was debilitating. No matter how hard I tried to fight it, I didn't have the skills or the abilities to win. I just didn't. I wasn't afraid to admit it. I needed to admit my failures. Being in denial and lying to myself is what I had done throughout our entire marriage. It had gotten me nowhere fast and I was now determined to leave.

I knew my children would suffer if I stayed. They needed to see what a healthy marriage looked like. They needed to know that it is not okay to accept abuse from anyone, including and especially your spouse or significant other. Being their first role model, I was not about to let them down. I never knew how good of an actress I was until I faked my marriage and sex and love. This was my only way out. I had to pretend nothing was different in order to make my escape. It took a lot of planning and preparation and I had to disguise my efforts behind a face of normalcy. I could not live with his abuse anymore. I had finally hit my breaking point. I had enough. I felt myself slowly fading away. There was a window of opportunity to make my move and I had to take it.

"Afraid of what?"

Her question had me erecting a fortress around my feelings. At this point, I wanted to tell her to fuck off too. It was clear to me the doctor had done her job. She was not needed anymore. She was the instrument I used to take the first step to leave my husband.

"I don't know." I said.

But at this point the truth didn't matter. I wasn't here to save my marriage. I was here to end it. Nick had worked me like I was a block of wood and he was the sculptor. He used his metaphorical chisel to remove the parts of me he didn't like. He whittled away until I was as close to his idea of perfection he could create. I don't think he ever loved me in my original state. I don't think he loved me in the transformation process either. I know he doesn't love me now and I doubt if he ever has.

She switched her questioning to Nick and I sat there in an unfamiliar daze as if my soul lifted from my body but I wasn't dead. The secret I'd been keeping was no longer suffocating me and I could breathe. It was ethereal, an instant cure for my angst. Nick's tears, words, and feelings were insignificant. He would get no empathy from me. His feelings didn't matter. My feelings toward him were cold and loathsome and I intended for them to stay that way. He wasn't going to get to me any longer and I participated minimally for the rest of the office visit. It mostly consisted of Nick crying and feeling sorry for himself and me fully checked out.

After the hour long session with the doctor was up, we scheduled another appointment. It was never my plan to attend again and we left somberly heading toward our separate vehicles. At home, it was eerily quiet and awkward while the kids were in school. We avoided each other for several hours orbiting around the house like planets. I was standing a little taller because the heaviness of my secret was no longer weighing on me. Nick was shriveled and weak, defeated from the sudden shock I delivered like a lightning bolt to his black heart.

My revelation came shortly afterwards as I contemplated what Dr. Lavalle had asked me. *Why didn't I tell him to fuck off? What was I afraid of?* The fear that consumed me was rooted in his ability to erase me from myself. I could feel my self-identity slipping away. He tricked me into believing the lies he told me about who I was. His plan unfolded gradually and unbeknownst to me, he would strip away my soul a little at a time. He would smile to my face and destroy me with his words and actions. He knew everything I was is all he would never be. Unable to bear the ache of the emptiness within, Nick callously pillaged from me. He wasn't heartless. He was soulless.

It was as if all of my positive traits and good personal attributes were being stuffed into an old, dusty chest in the attic. It's very sad to see yourself disappear. You can actually feel it happening. You reach for yourself. You watch as the weak version of yourself just walks away, brainwashed by some outside force while following some strange voice in the distance. You want to scream. You want to rescue yourself. But you don't know how. You are completely powerless. The shell of yourself just turns to look at you with blank eyes as she becomes more and more translucent, like a heartbroken ghost crossing over to the other side.

How could I let her go so easily? How could I not save her? It was only then when I finally realized she was not gone forever, just lost. I decided to find her. I would bring her back. I would seek out all of those wonderful parts of her again. Everything that was locked away in that attic would return: strength, determination, wisdom, and empathy. I was hell bent on finding her and decided, when I did, I would put all those pieces back together.

Nick failed to realize that by dimming my light, he was actually making me stronger. I had to fight harder and harder to make my light shine brighter. He was the rain as I tried to keep my fire burning, tirelessly attempting to shield and protect what was left of the soaking embers. But I was persistent. Giving up wasn't an option. Nick didn't know that it was impossible to take someone else's light. What he saw in me, he craved for himself. He knew he could never become what he wanted, so he sought out to steal it from me. Unfortunately for Nick, the soul doesn't work like that.

Things between us would never be the same after the therapy session. He knew I had one foot out the door. Nick was on high alert and panic-stricken, and I knew I could leave him. He would do whatever he needed to do in useless attempts to keep me from leaving. His efforts became overt and outlandish, likened to things he did at the beginning of our courtship. I felt broken, defeated, and lifeless. He'd proven to me by his actions that he didn't truly care about me over the years. Believing he could change now, for me, was impossible. Regrettably, it was too little, too late.

CHAPTER 27

MARRIED – 17 YEARS, 6 MONTHS

"Good morning," he said, softly waking me from my sleep. He was next to my side of the bed with a mug full of coffee. I blinked my eyes and sat up slowly.

"Oh, thanks." I said gruffly.

My throat was on fire. *A cold is coming on.*

I was still groggy and quite surprised by the gesture. He sat the big ceramic cup full of the aromatic brew on the nightstand and left the room sheepishly, like an abused servant. *Oh, the irony.* The steam danced like sheer curtains in a breeze. Hot coffee didn't appeal to my senses upon waking up with a sore throat. I didn't want his gift. It was too late. *How comical. He thinks he can just bring me a coffee after all of this.* Maybe he deserved some credit for trying, but the effort was long overdue. Because he was desperate for me to stay, he began to try something new.

Something he hadn't done since we first started dating. That 'something' was kindness.

Kindness was all I ever wanted from him. Finally, he was treating me how I wanted to be treated and he erroneously thought I would stay. He didn't know I was already emotionally checked out. I had already decided I didn't love him anymore. I buried my face into my pillow and went back to sleep. The coffee turned cold, just like my love for him.

Later in the afternoon, Nick and I pretended everything was normal between us. We agreed not to upset the kids or alert them to anything unusual. We briefly discussed doing it this way, and it seemed to flow properly and made it easier on everyone. Nick had been doing a complete turnaround. He was doing chores around the house, asking me if he could help me and trying to take on way more than he ever had.

"I'll get that," he said as he took a clean plate from my hands as I emptied the dishwasher. I didn't resist. I began to allow him to do as much as he wanted. It was nice for a change. You could say I was taking advantage of the situation since I knew deep down, I would still divorce him, regardless of any effort he put forth. But I didn't care. I continued to allow him to cook and clean and take care of all the things he demanded of me in the past.

The change was a bit frightening. He was not at all the same person I had known. He was clearly very afraid. After dinner was finished, he pulled out a gallon of ice cream for dessert. Coffee flavored.

I tried so hard to contain my laughter. I turned my face away from him and bit my lips between my teeth. *Does he think this is all about coffee? For God's sake! This is not about coffee. He has no idea what to do. He's completely pathetic.*

My first instinct was to take some and eat it. It would make him feel better. I quickly squashed the idea and politely refused. His gifts were too late and now unwanted. How many times could he have done something nice for me over all those years? He didn't care about me. He had multiple opportunities to do simple things for me and he chose not to and it disgusted me. Undelivered promises and lies were continual letdowns. My husband feared losing his grip on me and all of the things he never did were being illuminated. Anything he had to offer me now would be rejected. It was disingenuous. It was an act. I didn't believe he had the capability to change forever. The efforts he made were temporary, and I had no intention of changing my mind.

"What's this?" I stared at a large box by the Christmas tree wrapped in shiny red paper.

"I hope you like it. It's for you. I thought you might like to open it early. I'm sure you'll want to use it. I think you're gonna like this," Nick stuttered and stammered nervously.

I started pulling at the wrapping paper until it tore off piece by piece. His eyes were eager as I slowly peeled the paper away. Underneath revealed a thick cardboard box, not lending any clues to the contents. I smiled trying to conceal my confusion for fear of upsetting him since I didn't know what to expect. Gifts from Nick were typically afterthoughts: little effort, little preparation, and little money spent. Wrapping was usually non-existent.

"I have no idea what this could be?"

He inhaled steadily, slowly, as if he were taking a draw of a cigarette, and waited to exhale. I sliced the tape of the box with my thumbnail and pulled open the flaps. Inside were four separate boxes of coffee pods nestled tightly inside. My initial reaction was to laugh. With the kids looking on, I decided to smile instead.

"Oh wow, coffee. Lots of it!"

"Merry Christmas, early." He smiled and released an exasperated sigh.

"Thank you." I said.

Gifts from Nick were typically very last minute with little effort. He made coupon cards with construction paper and crayons the kids had fetched for him. Nick's cards closely resembled cards from one of my children, stick figures and all. Not to mock his artistic ability, rather, I'm highlighting the fact that Nick's gifts to me were the black and white Kansas to my colorful, sparkling OZ. My gifts for him required weeks of thought and days of planning. Still, they were not good enough for Nick. He fully expected me to be happy with handmade, childish looking cards with non-tangible gifts attached with future redemption. It was complete hypocrisy. I might have been able to overlook this without resentment if my daily life with Nick was pleasant. It wasn't.

Since I knew the drill, I obliged. I lifted the coffee pods from the box and expressed my gratitude by admiring all of the different flavor combinations he'd chosen.

"This is great. But I don't have a Keurig for them."

"That's okay, you'll get one later. I told my mom you'll need one."

Outwardly, I was excited. Deceptively, I was using him. My plan was to continue to take from him just as he took from me. Anything he offered me, I was going to accept. When he said I should sit while he cleaned up dinner, I sat. When he told me to get a relaxing bath while he put the kids to bed, I relaxed. When he offered to buy me the new SUV I'd been begging for years to have, I accepted. This was temporarily symbiotic. He thought he was buying me back into the marriage and I played along, knowing full well I was going to take everything I could and run.

I'd been pretending to be invested in this marriage since our visit with the therapist. Nick knew I wasn't one hundred percent devoted, so he was on his best behavior. He wasn't fully aware of me being completely checked out and just biding my time until after Christmas. Each day dragged by so slowly. I put the kids and myself to bed early every night just to make the morning come sooner. *Three more weeks. It's only three more weeks.* I kept my eyes on the prize. *If I can make it 17 years, I could make it 21 more days.*

Splitting up our family right before the holiday would be cruel to my children. If it weren't for them, I would have ripped the Band-Aid off much sooner. I wanted their last Christmas with all of us together to be a pleasant memory. Leaving them with worry and anxiety about their future in the days leading up to the happiest day of their year would break my heart.

While I wrapped Christmas gifts for the kids on the floor of our bedroom, Nick laid in bed watching sports on TV. Though I wasn't an expert at identifying narcissistic tactics at this stage of my awakening, I knew something about what he was about to say was inherently wrong.

"So, things are going really well lately, huh?"

His affirmative statement followed by a small question to encourage my interaction.

"What do you mean?" I asked.

"Well, I just think things are really positive for us lately."

"Oh. I'm not sure I agree."

"Well, but you're happy and things are better. I just think you need to realize things are actually really good between us lately. I've been a really good husband and things are not as bad as what you think they are."

As I sat there silently cutting and taping the brightly colored paper over the boxes of toys and clothing I realized what he was doing. Nick was making his best effort to make me think and feel what he wanted again.

"Nick, I know how I feel and I'm just not in agreement with you."

He kept pressing. He wanted me to go along with his fabrication and I refused. Maybe I was putting on such a good show for him and he actually believed things were turning around instantaneously. Or maybe he was attempting to control me through manipulation. Nick was unaware my mind was consumed with anxiety and I was afraid. My weight was at an all time low and I chugged water just to erase the sick feelings in my stomach. The only thing I thought about was protecting my children and me. The news of me actually following through with divorce would shock Nick. He was suspicious, but I don't think he ever thought I was capable of actually leaving. I sincerely doubt he ever thought I'd have the courage to go. Just a few months prior, I'd drunkenly blurted out that I wanted a separation. Unbeknownst to him, I actually wanted a divorce.

Unknowing how he might react, I decided it was dangerous and irresponsible to tell him I was divorcing him in person. My exit plan was ready. I lined up a place to go and I made sure it happened when I had the children in my care. Once I felt like my plan was safe and sound, I pulled the rug right out from under my husband, and my kids.

CHAPTER 28

THE SEPARATION – YEAR 17, MONTH 7

The parking lot was completely empty except for the sleek, new SUV Nick bought me. I arrived early to pick up the kids from school. Little snowflakes drifted toward the blacktop, melting upon contact. Perfectly unique clusters of delicate crystals falling to their demise and all I could do was watch them die. Their beauty was overshadowed by their bravery. They seemed to know this was just a part of their cycle and accepted it with ease, gliding down, faithfully knowing they would rise again.

I glanced at the clock on my dashboard. The kids wouldn't be let out from school for another forty-five minutes, plenty of time for me to disrupt Nick's world. I wrestled with my coat and scarf, ripping them off of me. It wasn't enough relief from the heat. With the simple push of a button, I slightly lowered the driver's side window and icy air gushed inside, immediately cooling me. Knowing I had to get this over with, I reached for my phone and opened my email to compose the single message I never thought I could send.

Parents were beginning to fill the empty spaces in the lot with their Escalades and BMWs. The snow was coming down faster and denser, creating a subtle white sheet marred with tire tracks. The clock was moving too fast. There were only thirty more minutes until the kids arrived.

Nick, I am taking the kids to my mom's house after school today. I will bring them back at bedtime. I filed for a divorce and my attorney needs to know where you want the papers sent. He can send them to your work, or to your attorney or have them hand delivered by the sheriff to the house. Let me know your preference. – Allison

My index finger hovered over the SEND button. My heart pulsed harder in my chest. There would be no turning back if I tapped it. My hand was shaking. I was millimeters away from doing one of the simplest yet hardest things I would ever do. *Just press SEND Allie. Do it. What are you so afraid of? He isn't here. Be brave.* There was no hesitation to take back my life, but fear of the unknown was crippling.

My three little reasons to push through would be my and their saving grace. But disappointing them and saving them wrestled in my heart. They were going to be devastated. They had no idea this was even a possibility. They wouldn't be expecting this whatsoever. I had to be sensitive to their feelings. They were at the forefront of my mind and I knew my choice to leave their father could leave an everlasting impact on their lives.

Any divorce is going to be hard, but I anticipated divorcing Nick would be the hardest thing I ever did. It took me a very long time to realize, understand, and accept that my husband was not who I thought he was. I couldn't imagine how totally impossible it might be for my little children to comprehend. I couldn't even explain it. *Would I be breaking their hearts? Would they blame me? Would they be able to adjust to a split family? Will they need therapy for years to come?*

Though I was afraid, I knew my children deserved to see what a respectful and happy marriage should be. They wouldn't know it now, but, in time, I hoped they would understand how they were such a huge part of my decision. They had to see the truth and I was the only one who could show it to them.

School had finally ended and the children were spilling from the double doors. It had to be now. *DO IT!* I squeezed my eyes shut hard, inhaled deeply and lightly tapped SEND.

I did it. My eyes widened, I exhaled and looked in my sent items to verify it had actually gone through. My heart raced. That little innocent SEND button turned me to stone. I was frozen. The message disappeared from my screen, but now it was on Nick's. My heart was thumping on my breastbone, trying to escape from my chest. Slowing my breathing didn't help. It was done. My stomach twisted in worry of how Nick would respond. *What would he do?* I wasn't sure of anything except this would be the beginning of the longest and arduous trek of my life. Surprisingly, Nick replied to my email within minutes.

You can send it to my attorney, Tim Shumann.

His response was simple. Not what I expected. *Maybe he didn't care. Maybe he wasn't shocked after all.* Regardless, I was relieved and happy he didn't fly into a fit of rage or insist I bring the kids home immediately.

When I neglected to turn down the street to our home, Claire noticed right away.

"Where are we going, Mom?" she asked.

"We're going to go to Nana's house to visit for a little while."

"Why? What for?"

"I'll let you know once we get there."

Claire's curiosity didn't lessen and ended up alerting Lleyton's as well. They both questioned me incessantly during the twenty minute drive to my mother's house a few cities away. Nervous energy was mounting within me.

My mom was waiting inside when we arrived with a look of compassion all over her face. She followed my lead, waiting for me to start the conversation. We all sat down on her large, plush sectional.

"Guys, I have something really important to tell you. This was a really hard thing for me to do and I know how confused you must be right now."

My voice cracked as I made an attempt to keep from crying.

"What's wrong, Mommy?!" Lleyton said. Her eyes flashed with fear.

"Guys, your dad and I are getting a divorce."

I didn't know how else to soften it. It just came out.

"No! Mommy! No!" Claire cried.

"What?! Why?!" Lleyton added and the tears began to fall.

My mom sat nearby, and Carter was on the floor playing with a deck of cards, seemingly unfazed.

"I will answer all of your questions and I'll tell you everything I can."

Lleyton jumped into my lap and curled up on me, crying. My heart was breaking.

Claire was shocked. I looked over at her and she stared lasers at me.

"I hate you! You ruined our life!" she screamed and ran up the stairs.

"I'll go," my mom said, and stood to go after her.

It was worse than I had expected. Delivering this news was excruciatingly painful. Never would I intentionally hurt my children, yet there was no denying I did. The pain I inflicted on my precious kids bounced right back to me. I cried when they cried. I hurt when they hurt. My parents divorced when I was around their ages and I too knew the sting of a family ripped in half.

Eventually the kids had calmed down after many questions and lots of tears. As promised, I took them back to their father before bedtime and left so he could have time with them alone. My heart was breaking for them, but it was me who did this. *Had I made the right decision? Would my kids ever forgive me?* It was an impossible position to be in. Trying to protect your children and hurting them at the same time.

For several months to come, I would bear the brunt of their suffering. When they blamed me, I accepted it. When they lashed out at me, I took it. When they begged me to go back to the marriage, I refused. Internalizing their hurt as my own was harder than I ever imagined it would be. Their emotional bullets pierced my heart, but I received each one after the other like any good mother would. It's what a strong parent does for their children. This wasn't their fault. It was Nick's for abusing me and it was mine for allowing it.

I would take the blame for the divorce even though he left our marriage years ago. He emotionally abused me and emotionally neglected me. I may have been the one who filed for divorce, but he left me well before our formal separation. The reality of the situation is that it never was a genuine marriage to begin with. It was a lie.

The two weeks between my email to Nick and the time I moved out of our house was spent searching for a place to live and avoiding Nick. We only spoke to each other out of necessity regarding the children. As usual, my days were spent at home while he worked but now my nights were spent sleeping over at Sasha's house. I left after the kids were in bed and I got up early and came back to the house before they were up for school.

I was still communicating with Johnny through Twitter and he told me some hard truths I hadn't previously considered.

Johnny: *You know this is far from over. You'll be dealing with him until Carter is 18. That's at least 10 more years. So don't get ahead of yourself too quickly. You left, and that was the first step, probably the hardest step, but you still have a long way to go. You cannot completely cut him off because he is the father of your kids. But you can distance yourself as much as possible avoiding his manipulation going forward. You need to stay true to yourself and remember how you got here. Don't look back. You did it. You freed yourself.*

His words permeated my thoughts. He was right. We shared custody of the kids and there was no way I could completely erase Nick from my life. I'd have to communicate with him periodically. I'd have to see him at sports activities and school functions. Our community was small and his family and their circle were big. I knew I would run into them and him on more than a few occasions. But making this transition as smooth as possible for my little ones was of utmost importance. They deserved sensitivity. They needed love from us both. They would need help from a therapist and I had to handle this in the best way I could.

Days before I officially moved into Sasha's, Nick offered to finish off the basement so I could live there so as not to disrupt the family. He said it was a 'thing' and divorced parents do this all the time. He called it 'parallel parenting.' This was as far from a possible option for me as I could imagine. I wanted to be as far away from him as I could.

"No. I do not want to live in this house," I told him directly.

What is he thinking? I am divorcing him. Why the hell would I want to be living in the same house!? Why would I want to subject myself to his prying eyes and controlling behaviors as a single mom?

Speaking my truth was becoming easier and easier. Maybe it was because I had already taken the first step, which I never thought I could. Maybe it was because the monster I once believed had power over me was reduced to a worm. Maybe it was both. In any case, it didn't really matter. Ultimately, I was on my way out of a toxic relationship and I wasn't looking back. The hardest part was getting the courage to leave, but the journey was just beginning.

CHAPTER 29

THE SEPARATION – YEAR 17, MONTH 8

Freedom wasn't fully mine yet and I was denied liberty for so long that a mere taste of it cultivated a craving inside me. I wanted more. I thought if I got far enough away from him, I could free myself from his control. Nick couldn't trap me in lectures anymore. He couldn't watch my every move and critique my actions and words. It was such a relief to breathe again. The one thing I didn't count on was freeing myself from his mental enslavement.

Physically, I was free, but, mentally and emotionally, I was still trapped. It followed me throughout my days like a shadowy stalker. It showed up in my dreams at night to taunt me. It triggered anxiety, depression, and fear using the slightest, most innocent events in my life. *How could I be so far away from Nick, yet still feel him controlling my life?* These mental shackles were not breaking easily. They'd been on for so long and I was afraid they were permanent and would never come off. I hated that he could still control me while not even in my presence. *This has to end. I will not allow him to have any more of me.*

Soon after leaving him, I learned that fully freeing myself was going to take time and lots of effort on my part. I wasn't going to be able to do it alone, so I immediately enlisted the professional help of a therapist named Connie Mitchell. I needed help. There was no denying it. The frustration was boundless as I fought to save myself every day. *Why am I thinking of what he wants? Why can't I go to dinner without having an anxiety attack? How can I start trusting other people? Will I ever feel normal again?* I blamed Nick for all of this uncertainty. *He did this to me.* The brokenness inside me was his fault, and I hated him for it. Nick's death was still at the top of my wish list because, in my mind, he wasn't ready to let me go.

"Hey, it's Mom. Um, I need to tell you something you're not going to believe."

My mom called me at 11:30 p.m. on a Wednesday night. I knew it had to be important.

"Is everything okay?" I asked.

"Everything is fine, but I'm kind of in shock. Nick just left my house."

"What? Nick? Why?"

My heart was racing, and I flung myself up from my bed. I was confused and afraid. *I'm going to kill him.* Nick sent handwritten letters to me through our kids' backpacks begging me not to end our marriage. He had recently reached out to my dad and stepmom, my brother, and some of my friends. He cried to them, pouring out his heart and trying to gain their sympathy. He had always treated my mom horribly, so I was shocked now too.

"He was here for two hours and. . ."

"Mom! You talked to him for TWO hours?!" I yelled through the phone in disbelief.

"Just listen to me. He scared me to death because it was 9:30, and I was in the backyard with the dog, and I saw this man coming around by the fence. It was dark outside, and I didn't know who it was. When I finally realized it was him, he was already in the yard with me."

"Well, what the hell did you talk about for two hours?!"

"Don't yell at me, just listen. I'll tell you the whole story. He had a bottle of bourbon and some ice cream with him. They were gifts for me. It was so weird. His eyes were all glassy like, and he looked like he was on something. I don't know for sure, but he could have been drunk or high or something. So, he asked me if we could talk, and I told him yes and to come inside the house." Her words flew out of her mouth, trying to get it all out as quickly as possible.

"Mom! Are you crazy?! You have no idea what he is capable of. The kids say he's on all kinds of prescription medications they've seen in his medicine cabinet. I know he's been drinking."

She interrupted my lecture.

"I don't know why I let him in. I just did. He cried in front of me. He apologized for treating me so badly over the years and for treating you so badly. He looked skinny and sickly. He looked really awful. I felt sorry for him."

Anger welled up within me. *He deserves no sympathy. This is all an act.* Nick thought he could manipulate my mother. I was waiting for her to tell me I should give him another chance.

"Oh, Mom, what did you do?"

"Well, I didn't accept the bourbon or the ice cream," she said proudly. "I just let him cry and talk."

Nick's desperation extended out like slimy tentacles across my life. He refrained from speaking to my mom, yet now was bringing gifts and sharing feelings. He was hoping to manipulate my mom so she would convince me to stay. This was too much. He was a loose cannon.

"Mom, do not ever engage with him again. Do not reply to texts, do not answer calls, and definitely do not let him in your house. My leaving, rocked his world. We have no idea how he could behave."

"Do you think he would hurt me? Hurt you?"

"I honestly have no clue. But it just isn't worth taking the chance."

After I hung up the phone, fear overcame me. *How can I be so afraid of someone I'd lived with and loved so long? Had children with. Shared a bed with. How can I be free of him and still enslaved?* The conflict between his mental hold on me and my physical distance from him was inevitable. It's not like he had superhuman powers to control me from afar. What he did have was years of conditioning me in which I produced the behaviors he wanted. I was still nothing but a servant. He was still the master. I knew I could be halfway across the world and Nick could still permeate my mind and affect my life with his poison. I was terrified of his mental games, but, more so, I was furious I'd allowed him to keep those hooks in me. Nick wasn't going to get away with this anymore. My determination was set into motion. Nick was a brain tumor inside my head, and I needed to be the surgeon to extract it.

The next morning, I went to go pick up the children from Nick where we used to share a home. My first mistake was entering the house. Nick was sitting in the recliner with his computer on his lap. I glanced around feeling disappointed in how neglected my beautiful home was since I'd left. Soiled dishes were balanced upon each other in the sink. Several dried up Cheerios were sticking to the granite countertop among crumbs and other random spills. Clothes and shoes were strewn along the carpet and particles of dirt and debris crunched beneath my shoes. *This is disgusting. How can he live like this? What has he done to my beautiful house?*

Nick stood from his chair and asked if he could speak to me privately. I hesitantly agreed.

"What's going on?" I asked as I followed him down the hallway towards the master bedroom.

He was carrying his laptop out in front of him and walked into the bedroom.

"Come in here, and we can shut the door and talk."

My pulse immediately began to race. *Don't tell me what to do.* I stood firmly in the hall, the doorframe between us both. *No. I will not be locked in a room with you.* I felt light-headed. *Allie, you know what you need to do.*

"What do you want to talk about?" I asked him.

"Can you just come in here so I can shut the door and talk to you?" he pleaded.

"No, tell me what you want to talk about."

He hesitated and sighed with disappointment.

"I wrote you an apology, and I want to read it to you."

"Well you can just email it to me. I don't need you to read it to me."

"Dr. Lavalle thinks I need to read it to you though, so can you just come in here please?"

His desperation reeked. My brows furrowed and my eyes squinted further and I could feel them peering at him, trying to discern what he was trying to pull over on me. There was no way in hell after leaving him that I was going to allow him to put me in a room so he could sob about all the things he did to me over the years just to try to get me to come back. *Email the apology, and then I can decide if I want to read it or not. Maybe I don't want to read your apology. Maybe you don't deserve that. Maybe I don't have to do anything you or your stupid doctor says.* I decided to stand my ground refusing to give into his demands.

"Well, I don't really care what Dr. Lavalle thinks. If you want me to read it, just email it to me."

Nick's face went pale, and he stood there staring at me like he was drowning, and I just refused to throw him a life vest. He shut the laptop, and I turned to go back into the kitchen. I rounded up the kids, and they piled into my SUV. Nick never did email his apology letter to me. It wouldn't have mattered anyway. I never intended to read it or any future apologies he would send me. He never had any real remorse, just regret he wouldn't be able to have the same easy life he had when I was there. My role regarding his abuse was not to make him feel better by listening to his confessions. It most definitely didn't require forgiveness. If and when I ever decide to forgive him, it would only be for me, and he will sure as hell never get the pleasure of knowing about it.

CHAPTER 30

THE SEPARATION – YEARS 17, MONTH 9

Weeks had gone by living at Sasha's house and sharing custody back and forth with the kids. The kids and I were settled in well and I was comfortable, physically, where I was. Routine kept me grounded, and my family and friends were extremely supportive and helpful. I was attending weekly sessions with my new therapist, Connie, and I was feeling all around calm and peaceful. She told me something I'd carry with me forever. It was something I hadn't considered before.

"Nick's family circle is toxic. You were a part of this toxicity until you broke away. Toxic people project their own fears and failures onto their victims. They have deep wounds that likely stemmed from childhood traumas that have caused them self-loathing. They despise these things and try to erase them by projecting and then attacking those things in others. They deny these traits in themselves refusing to accept it is they who possess them."

My mind was clear, and my emotions were stable. I was relaxing on the couch, peaceful and calm. Nothing could touch me. Nothing could affect me. I went to therapy regularly. I read self-help books. I subscribed to podcasts and YouTube videos on healing from abuse. True healing takes time and I was getting ahead of myself. But, as I'd soon find out about healing, more than time, it takes work.

The kids were with Nick, and Sasha was out of town. I had the house to myself. While nodding off, my serenity was ripped from my grip like a purse snatcher. The alarming ding of a text notification came through on my phone. It was Sasha. I switched the notifications to vibrate and closed my eyes. The phone vibrated four more times. My serenity was interrupted in a formidable way I couldn't have predicted.

This must be important. I opened the texts. On my phone's screen were several pictures of Nick and a young woman, together.

> **Sasha:** *Is this Nick? Who is this girl he's with and why is he in Nashville?*

> **Allison:** *Yes, that's him. I have no idea who she is. He told the kids he was going on a work trip.*

> **Sasha:** *LOL – well they don't appear to be working. He is very into her and I saw him kiss her on the forehead.*

> **Allison:** *What a POS. I hate him. He's already doing out of town overnight trips with other women?*

> **Sasha:** *How do you know its overnight?*

> **Allison:** *Because I saw Air BNB charges and concert tickets purchased on the credit card. I can see everything he is spending money on because we are still sharing finances until the divorce is final. He's been*

spending thousands of dollars on alcohol and Uber rides too.

Sasha: *Wow! Thousands? He must really be on a downward spiral.*

Allison: *Yep. He goes out constantly. I track everything on a spreadsheet. He's up to $4000.00 in alcohol and designated driving. Did he see you there?*

Sasha: *No. I don't think so. But I got a really good look at her. And she's not nearly as pretty as you.*

Allison: *Thanks girl. Love you! Enjoy the concert. We can chat later.*

I zoomed in on the picture, studying her facial profile and her unmistakable arm sleeve tattoo. She was naturally very pretty and clearly much younger than him. Anger burned me from the inside. Nick had never taken me to a concert before, not even a local one. *Why wasn't I worth taking to a concert? What was so special about this girl? Why did he dote on her?* It was unfair. I was jealous. It was a strange feeling because I hate Nick. Not one tiny cell of my body was interested in being with him. But the injustice of him treating some girl he barely knew infinitely better than me, his wife, stung like a slap across my face.

It didn't take Nick long to move on from me leaving. He attempted pretty seriously to get me back and to get me to change my mind. Once he figured out it was a lost cause, he was ready to begin dating. Shortly after I filed for divorce from my husband, his Amazon search history revealed gifts for women, condoms and a big, black 18" dildo. *Who knew Amazon sold condoms and dildos?*

Upon inspecting our credit card transactions, I could see his shocking transformation right before my eyes. He bought a gym membership and began taking workout supplements. He bought hundreds of dollars of trendy clothing, shoes, sunglasses, and accessories during this time. He began consulting with Jenny to help him buy things to improve his appearance. It didn't take long to recognize he was love bombing this girl. He was doing the exact thing to her as he did to me at the beginning of our relationship.

Right away I searched for some clues on social media. I didn't have any idea who I was looking for, so I started with Nick. He never liked the idea of social media and hated when I used it. He refused to have any accounts and refused to take pictures with me to post on my pages. As I searched his name, my suspicions were right. My husband, who was always anti-social media, had a Facebook, an Instagram, and a Pinterest account.

I'll be damned. I was shocked. In disbelief, I pulled my phone closer to my face. *Holy shit! Nick has social media!* Each of his accounts was set to private, and I was unable to get any information. The next logical step was to look through his friend's accounts. I'm embarrassed to admit I spent hours and hours digging through his friends' accounts looking for anything I could find. It became obsessive for me to uncover something – anything to reveal some details about the mystery girl in the picture. By the end of the night, all I was left with was frustration, exhaustion, and sore eyes from staring at my phone.

A few days later, Nick had dropped off the kids at my house and they came in, barreling me with hugs, kisses, and stories to share.

"Mommy, what is swing dancing?" Claire asked.

"Oh, it's a fun type of dance where a man flips and spins a woman around on the dance floor."

"Mom, I think Dad is trying to replace you," Claire said, very seriously.

"Oh? Why do you think that?" I asked.

"Well, I overheard him telling Meemaw he was going to start taking swing dancing lessons with some girl named Hannah. They didn't know I was listening, so I asked him who Hannah was."

"Well, who is she?"

"He said she's just a friend, but I don't believe him."

My imagination started envisioning a class of men throwing women overhead, splits and fast feet. Then I saw Nick making a valiant effort to impress a naive woman who appreciated his two left feet and nervous laughter. It was comical to me. He would appear to enjoy swing dancing, but deep inside he would hate it. It was simply a tactic to lure in a new victim. He would give her what she wanted and, when she got hooked, he could put her in his cage where he wanted her.

I was envious of Nick. I saw him enjoying life, meeting new people and accumulating nice things. All of these outward actions were a result of a broken person trying to fill an empty hole. Where once it was me who filled this gap, now it was many other things. When I decided to remove myself from an abusive life with Nick is when the wound reopened in him. There was a black, gaping hole in his reality I left behind after I was gone. Nick's fear and self-loathing exposed itself every morning when he opened his eyes. I imagined indescribable pain washing over him from a void where there once was soothing relief. The relief was at the expense of my soul. But it didn't matter to him. All that mattered to him was feeling better. Much like a drug addict coming down from a high, just like Johnny described. The only thing on Nick's mind was getting the next fix.

"You said her name is Hannah?" I asked to clarify.

"Yeah, I bet she's his girlfriend, and he's trying to replace you Mom. What do you think?"

"I think you, my sweet, are a very smart girl."

She smiled revealing her perfectly straight teeth, and her pretty, brown eyes shined the color of acorns in the sunlight.

"You're awfully cute, too," I said, winking at her as I wiped down the kitchen table.

While the kids played, I mindlessly cleaned the house and thought about Hannah. The excitement of finding out who she was tugged at my curiosity. As soon as I finished my chores and the kids were tucked into bed, I started more obsessive investigating on social media. It was exceptionally difficult to find this girl without a last name. I searched on friend lists for any person named Hannah I could find. It never came up with a match to the girl in the picture. This felt impossible, but I kept searching.

"Mom! I left my soccer shoes at Dad's house on the back porch!" Lleyton came running down the hallway in a panic.

"Honey, it's okay. I can run over there tonight and get them for you."

She immediately relaxed and jumped on me to give me a hug. We squeezed each other tightly.

"Thank you, Mommy! I love you so much."

"I love you, too, sweetheart, now back in bed."

What I didn't realize as I watched my curly haired daughter skip down the hall was that her forgetting her uniform would lead me to another clue. It was going to be a very big help in unlocking the mystery of who Hannah was.

CHAPTER 31

THE SEPARATION – YEAR 17, MONTH 10

he first thing I saw when I pulled up the driveway to my former home was a rusted, silver Kia I didn't recognize. It didn't appear Nick was home, but someone he knew left a car in the driveway. I went straight to the vehicle and tried to open the doors. *Locked, damnit.* At least a registration or something inside might have given me some evidence of who it belonged to. I noticed a lot of trash and clothing strewn about. The items inside didn't provide any clues if this car belonged to a man or a woman. Instead of giving up, I snapped a picture of the license plate, walked to the porch to get Lleyton's shoes and went home.

The entire drive I kept questioning myself. *Why do you even care? You left HIM, remember?* It didn't really make sense to me, but, by this point, I had already gotten enough information to make some headway, so I didn't stop. I immediately thought of my old friend, Bill, a retired police officer who might still have access to the database. I sent the picture of the license plate and texted him right away.

Allison: *Hey Bill, sorry to bother you. I know you are retired from the force now, but is there any chance you might still have access to run this plate for me and see who the car is registered to?*

Bill: *Yeah, no problem. Looks like it is registered to a man named Frank Jackson, his address is 8398 Train Station Rd. Do I even want to know what you're going to do with this information?*

Allison: *The car is in my driveway and I'm just trying to figure out who it belongs to.*

Bill: *Ahhh. Ok. Well if you need any other help, just let me know!*

Allison: *Thank you so much!*

I felt like I'd just won the lottery! Excitement rushed through me, and I couldn't wait to get started cyber stalking.

Frank Jackson. I thought. There were so many of them out there on social media. The name was so common it might as well have been a needle in a haystack. I scoured the local Frank Jackson's social media accounts. I inspected all his young female followers for hours, jotting down notes so I didn't backtrack into a spot of the maze I'd already been. It took me almost a full week to connect all of the dots, but, after much persistence, I discovered Hannah was Frank Jackson's daughter. The girl in the picture with Nick at the concert was now exposed. My obsessive digging paid off. Even though most of her social media was private, I was still easily able to learn a lot about her.

From my new discovery, I learned she was just twenty-three years old, full of life and beauty. The deep dive online was enlightening. She was a nature-loving, outdoorsy, pet sitter who traveled the world and lit up a room when she walked in.

For a few minutes, I just stared at her face on my screen. She was youthful and glowing. She wore very little makeup and was naturally beautiful. The small diamond stud in her nose and two dimples on her cheeks accentuated her face. But the longer I stared, the sooner I noticed something eerily familiar in her bright blue eyes. They sparkled with life and joy. They were innocent and inquisitive. They were hopeful and optimistic, just like mine used to be. Hannah was me, many years ago. Thoughts wrestled with each other in my mind: *Snap out of it. She's banging your husband. But she can't help it. He's a con artist. Don't feel bad for her! She's a young naive girl. She's stupid! I do feel bad for her. She doesn't want to be controlled and manipulated by him. I could help her. You cannot help her. Even if you told her what he is, she would never believe you. She would think you are trying to get him back!* I sighed, knowing only one of my voices in contention was right.

Nick deserved to die. *Who does he think he is, doing this to women?* He forced me to own vengeance as a personality trait and I hated it. It's a villainous trait, not one of an honorable person. I didn't want to be the villain in my own story. I knew who the true villain was, and it wasn't me. I wanted Nick to suffer as he made me suffer. I wanted him to feel sadness, loss, hurt, anger, frustration, and isolation. Not because I'm jealous he's with other women, but solely because he didn't deserve to be happy for one second of his pathetic life. *Why should he get away with tricking another unsuspecting woman?*

I envisioned him smiling his 'good guy' smile. I saw him sweet-talking his way into trust and familiarity. I saw kisses on the forehead and gentle brushes of her fingertips. I saw lavish gifts and a woman's eyes sparkling like the diamond he put on my finger all those years ago. And I also saw right through all of his bullshit.

Nick seemed happy. This was the root of my anger. He wasn't truly happy, just temporarily getting the fixes he needed. I quickly realized Nick would never be happy unless he was victimizing someone else. He would never fully feel whole unless he felt superior to others, tearing them apart as he did to me. He couldn't reach happiness unless it was at someone else's expense.

I've come to terms that I'm not a hero. Even if I tried to interfere, the veil is so thick with lies that she'd never believe me. I'd be pegged as jealous or regretful for leaving him. As much as I didn't want anyone to suffer the way I did, I realized their journey is their own and I cannot interfere. Not only was it not my place, but it was also not my responsibility. I am only responsible for my children and me. This went against my instincts. Putting others before me is what I do. It's who I am. But I also realized it's exactly what got me into this position to begin with.

Hannah would have to learn her own lessons in her own time, just like me. Guilty thoughts began to creep in. *This is wrong. Cyber stalking her is invasive. Why do I even care? I feel bad for her, yet I'm purposefully violating her personal life.* Guilt. More Guilt. *Stop it, Allie. Get a hold of yourself.*

Instantly, my sadness for Hannah and self-inflicted guilt turned to hatred for Nick. I was seething inside. I was hurt, I was furious, and I was feeling spiteful. I wanted to strangle him with my bare hands and watch the life slip out of his body. *God, why can't he just die?* At minimum, I wanted to hurt him or severely embarrass him. I wanted him to know what I knew, and I hoped he hated it.

I had an idea full of spite and revenge. Abruptly, I switched gears, closed down the social media and went to work on Amazon.com. Since we still shared an account, I went to the site in hopes he would see my purchases and browsing history. The first thing I found was a book called *I Hope You Die* and a t-shirt with the words YOU SUCK across the front. There was an adult coloring book titled *I Hate My Ex-Husband.* I put all of it in my cart. It all had to be mine. 'Click, click, Add to Cart.' *Oh, how I love you Amazon!* The fun in this quickly put out the flames of hatred I was harboring.

Before I knew it, I was laughing out loud and giddy with excitement, punching away at the keys on my computer. The best purchase I made was a set of temporary tattoo arm sleeves just like Hannah's for sixteen dollars. When the tattoos arrived in the mail, I innocently encouraged my unaware daughters to apply them to their arms in the exact placement as the mystery woman in the photos. Inside, I was laughing with hysteria like a cackling witch over a bubbling cauldron. I couldn't wait for Nick to see these fake tattoos on our pre-teen girls. This would definitely embarrass him. The girls didn't know about Hannah's tattoos, but I knew when his mother saw them, she would disapprove, further driving the embarrassment wedge deep into Nick's heart of coal.

Nick pulled into the driveway, and the kids and I walked outside. The girls, in tank tops, approached his car with their skinny, little arms exposing bold fake tattoos.

"Hey, nice tattoos," he said, feigning a compliment.

"I had inspiration," I said with an exaggerated roll of my eyes.

This was a childish game. I will be the first to admit this. Being passive aggressive and immature aren't good character traits, but, right then, it was definitely better than the alternative dream I had of shooting him in the face. It was soothing and made my pain just a little more bearable. It doesn't excuse the behavior. It doesn't make me any less petty. I felt it was harmless and completely deserved for all he had put me through. Ultimately, it made me feel a brief sense of victory over the villain I despised.

After the kids and Nick pulled away, my satisfaction faded, and my anger didn't subside. I couldn't shake it. There was a tidal wave of emotions pulling me in the undertow. *How can I hurt him? What can I do to not get into trouble and hit him where it hurts? How can I make him pay for what he's done?* A scream was emerging within my throat. It wanted out like a caged lion.

"Pay!" I screamed out loud. "That's it! Fuck you, Nick, I'm going shopping!"

Ulta Beauty was my first stop. Perfume, make-up, vitamins, and teeth whitening, altogether racked up a nice $400.00 charge. Nick was stingy with his money, so his wallet was where I knew I could hit him where it hurt the most. I paid for the items for the girl in line in front of me. She almost cried when she thanked me.

"You don't know this, but you're actually helping me," I told her. "I've been really angry today, and I needed to do something nice for somebody so I can feel not so hateful."

Afterwards, I went to Victoria's Secret, a jewelry store, and a host of other places to spend money. I shopped without looking at prices and swiped our joint credit card like it was my job. My warpath around town was blazing and so was the anger inside me. *He needed to pay more.* The hundreds of dollars I'd spent would get his attention but wouldn't be enough to piss him off. I had to think of something bigger.

When I got home, Sasha was lying on the couch watching television. I plopped down and told her everything.

"Allie, get online and buy yourself a Louis Vuitton purse! You've always wanted one. Just do it!"

I'd never spent such and exorbitant amount of money on a single accessory in my life. Typically, a twenty-five dollar purse from Target or something used from Goodwill was all I was brave enough to buy.

"Oh my God! That's a great idea! It will show up instantly on the credit card, too! You're a genius."

As I scanned the website for the purse I wanted, I realized that I had no idea how expensive these purses were. My eyes opened wide as I looked at the extra zeros at the end of the numbers.

"Sasha, twelve-hundred dollars?! These are way more than I thought. I don't know if I can."

"Yes, you can. And you can always return it if you decide against it. But, you know, it would be the ultimate 'fuck you' to that horrible man. You deserve that purse and he deserves revenge!"

She was right. It was time to show Nick who I was. He needed to see I wasn't playing around. He needed to know I had my own power, and I could make my own decisions. My cursor hovered over the button to place my order.

"Do it. You can do it!" She squealed.

After a brief hesitation, I winced, I clicked, and I became the new owner of the most expensive purse I'd ever bought.

"Haha! I did it! I bought it! I feel better!" I laughed.

"Maybe there's something to be said for retail therapy after all!" Sasha laughed.

"Nick is going to lose his shit when he sees this," I said.

"Well, he can't say a damn thing about it. He's been going out spending thousands of dollars on fancy dinner dates and bars with his whores. You should have bought two more!" We laughed hysterically together.

"You're right. I don't even care. But I do want my lawyer to be prepared because, tomorrow morning, you know he's going to get a call from Nick's lawyer. I don't want it to catch him off-guard."

"That's smart.".

My attorney, Vince, replied to my text shortly after I explained my lavish purchase.

> **Vince:** *Wow! That is actually hilarious. The girls in the office are going to have a field day with this.*

> **Allison:** *I'm so relieved you think it's funny. I was a little worried it might be a problem.*

> **Vince:** *Nope. Not a problem at all.*

His reaction didn't surprise me. Vince knew all about Nick and his abusive behaviors. He knew Nick obsessively checked his "net worth" daily, watching it grow. He knew Nick was financially abusive and controlled my spending during the marriage. But we were on status quo and the law said during the separation, my money was his and his money was mine. Until we were officially divorced, there would be nothing to stop Nick or me from spending the money however we saw fit.

> **Allison:** *Well Nick is going to flip out as soon as he sees this transaction on the credit card statement. I just*

wanted you to be prepared for his lawyer to ask you about it.

Vince: *Don't worry. He can't say a thing about it considering all the spending he's been doing. Of which you haven't complained once.*

Nick was so predictable. He went straight to his attorney, just like I knew he would. Vince replied to a gentle reminder from Nick's lawyer that I shouldn't be spending so much money.

I smiled from ear to ear reading Vince's immediate response.

"Mr. Shumann, My client will reel in her spending as soon as your client stops his spending, of which over $4000.00 has been in alcohol and Uber rides, over 2/3 of my client's purchase."

These types of little wins kept me motivated to persevere. I was thrilled with Vince's swift and accurate reply. This was nothing new to me. Nick spent whatever he felt was justified during our marriage while simultaneously questioning if my purchases were valid. It was nothing for him to purchase an eight-hundred dollar crossbow he would hunt with one time. Meanwhile, if I needed a new purse, spending over twenty-five dollars would be considered excessive in his mind. Naturally, me purchasing a well-known, brand-name, luxury handbag was going to make his head explode, and he could do nothing about it.

The purse arrived in the mail within a few days. I set the box on my bed and carefully lifted it out.

"Well, aren't you pretty!" I said aloud.

I slipped my arm through the straps and settled them on my shoulder. It felt strange carrying something of so much value on my arm. *I'm not sure I can even wear this in public. What if I lose it? What if someone steals it?* Honestly, it was a bit scary for me. After admiring its quality for a few minutes, I laid it on my bed, took a picture of it and posted it on my SnapChat story with some adorable, excited emojis. This was a purposeful and calculated move on my part. It wasn't just a normal post on a story for no reason except to brag about my new purse. I knew who looked at my stories and I knew there would be a leak back to Nick about it. As I expected, a few hours later, I received a notification that my sister-in-law, Jenny, had taken a screenshot of my purse picture. I waited patiently, knowing, very soon, something else would occur. And it did.

The next day, Jenny texted me and asked how I got the purse.

It seemed like an odd question to me. I considered different responses to the question, *"Oh, I picked it up at Goodwill." "My friend gifted her old one to me." "I borrowed it." "I won it on a radio show contest."*

It made me laugh. That one question was a tell-all for the financial abuse I dealt with. I responded like any self-sufficient, independent woman would.

Allison: *I bought it.*

Jenny never replied. From there, it was clear to me Nick's family was using Jenny. They all knew she was the closest to me, and they were getting information from her each time Jenny and I spoke. Jenny was hurting. I knew she was sad I decided to leave Nick. She had previously told me she missed me, and I missed her too. But Jenny and I were drifting apart for a few, key reasons. I was no longer in the same space mentally, emotionally, and even physically as Jenny. To protect her, I had to distance myself from her. The entire Adrian family was always going to use her as long as they could get away with it. They tried to get to me in other ways, but I easily shut them down. Jenny was their pawn. She didn't know it, but I certainly did. I know I broke Jenny's heart, but I could see no other way for me to keep them from pulling her strings and using her unfairly like they did. She would always be used, whether she knew it or not. Jenny was their mole. She was the informant for the other team and a spy for my enemy. By eliminating that possibility, I kept her out of the war zone.

CHAPTER 32

THE SEPARATION – YEAR 17, MONTH 11

nswer the damn phone, Nick! My frustration was building as I reached his voice message for the third time. I cringed upon hearing the gruff ejaculation of his mumbled words. I hung up and dialed again.

"Come on you guys. We have to go. Get in the car!" I barked at the kids.

"But I don't have my soccer cleats!" Claire said, panicked.

"I know! We're going to go over to your dad's house and get them. Let's go."

Claire, Lleyton, and Carter tossed their soccer bags and water bottles into the trunk and hurried into the car, following my lead of urgency. We had three games ahead of us and were down a pair of cleats. Keeping track of all the kids' school items and sporting gear was an adjustment for them and for me. They transferred things back and forth from Nick's house to mine and, inevitably, something would be forgotten or lost.

"You are speeding Mom," Carter said.

"Honey, we have to get the cleats from your dad's house and then make it to the first game on time!"

I sped along the old familiar curves with ease. Claire grabbed the handle on the car door bracing herself as we took the bends. My eyes were wide while I scanned the area for cop cars on the way to the place I used to call home. A speeding ticket now would further slow us down. *He is so inconsiderate. What if this was an emergency? He's probably sleeping off a hangover from the night before. Maybe he's dead. Hopefully he's dead.*

I pushed the pedal hard, speeding up the long driveway. My heart sunk into my stomach as soon as I saw it. *What should I do? Should I park? Should we go in? Should I turn around and leave? Now I know why Nick wasn't answering my calls.* There in front of us was the same silver car I saw the last time I was here.

My face grew hot. My breathing became rapid and, before I knew it, I had slammed the gearshift into park and was jumping from the car.

"Well, come on, let's go meet your dad's girlfriend. Carter, stay in the car."

I pressed the garage door opener in my car and before it was fully up, Claire was inside. Lleyton and I followed behind her as she punched in the alarm code to disarm it. The three of us marched into the kitchen just as Nick came flying out of the bedroom. His eyes were large with shock. He stood in the pathway to the bedroom, bare-chested in a pair of boxer shorts. I looked around for Hannah. *She must be hiding.* The only thing I saw was a fat purse spilling over with clutter. It sat on the kitchen barstool like a lazy cat. I had no idea what I was looking for, but I began digging through it erratically, flinging random things onto the floor. Claire walked over to Nick and he blocked her from passing.

"Dad, why won't you let me pass?" Claire asked.

He held her shoulders preventing her from going toward the bedroom. She continued to try and go around him, but he was determined to hide whoever was beyond the hallway.

"Yeah, Nick. Why won't you let her pass? Who's back there?" I asked, sarcastically.

He and I locked eyes. The fury in my gaze was so intense I thought I might set him ablaze. I would have loved to watch him burst into flames.

"Why don't you ask him whose car is in the driveway? Oh, and why don't you ask him whose purse this is?"

I pointed to the disorganized mess on the chair.

"Allie, please don't do this," he said in the calmest voice he could.

My adrenalin was pumping through my veins, and my anger erupted like a volcano.

"You couldn't even wait until we were fucking divorced?!" I screamed.

Lleyton began to cry.

"Mommy, you said a bad word."

"Come on, let's go," I snapped.

I fumed out of the house and grabbed Lleyton's hand, pulling her behind me. We got into the car and waited for Claire. My emotions were chaotic. There was anger, fear, betrayal, hurt, and sadness. Lleyton could sense the tension. She reached up to me from the back seat and hugged me around the neck. We squeezed each other for a long time, and I realized how much scandal she had just witnessed.

"I'm so sorry," I cried, "you shouldn't have had to see that. I shouldn't have let you go in there."

"It's okay Mommy. I love you."

From my peripheral vision, I saw Claire and Nick walk out of the house together.

Carter saw him and yelled, "Daddy!"

I rolled down my window to try to eavesdrop on their conversation, but we were too far away. She amazed me with her strength. She stood there, questioning her father, holding him accountable for his lies of omission and inconsistencies of his actions and words. She needed to ask him the hard questions, and he needed to be held accountable, so I allowed it for a short time.

"We need to go, Claire," I shouted through the window. My voice quivered as I restrained myself from releasing my emotions.

It was time to go. I had enough of my thoughts, of his face, and of the drama. He disgusted me. I wanted to leave. Nick walked back inside the house and Claire hopped into the passenger seat.

"There's no game today, Mom," she said.

"What? How do you know?" I asked.

"Dad said there was an email this morning and they cancelled it because the field was too wet."

My forehead slumped onto the steering wheel. I hadn't checked my email before we left. *Damn it.* Had I known the game was cancelled I would have never come over here looking for soccer cleats. The entire dramatic event for my children and me could have been avoided. *You fucked up.* Intense emotions led to errors in my judgment as I inserted my kids and myself into Nick's personal business. There was no justification other than I was overcome with outrageous foreign feelings. A delicate touch from my daughter was just the sweet consolation I needed.

"It's okay, Mom."

"I'm so sorry, you guys."

Tears began to drip down my cheeks as I hid my face from my children. *I'm so tired of crying. I'm so tired of feeling this way.* To the outside world, my turmoil was hidden behind a well-put together face. There were no visible cuts, bruises, or broken bones. Yet emotional abuse still imprinted those invisible scars that would remain in me forever. Within me, there was evidence of love bombs, verbal lashings, and emotional bruises. Defeat from mental mixed martial arts left me stunned. The unfair fighting with lies and manipulation left me crippled and weak, and there were stabbings to my character and strangulation of my soul. These kinds of wounds can never be seen with the eye. When tears leave scars, they are left on the heart.

CHAPTER 33

THE SEPARATION – YEAR 18

The tangled mess of emotions within me sent me into a whirlwind of despair.

"I hate Nick. I don't want to be with him. I left HIM. Why do I feel like this?" I cried.

Connie listened intently as I replayed the entire span of events to her. The feelings were just as real, replaying them, as they were when they happened. It was still raw. It was still hurting. But it made no sense to me. Jealousy should be the furthest thing from my mind. But it wasn't. *Move on, Nick. Go abuse someone else. Leave me alone. I really don't give a flying fuck what you do.* Pinpointing the source of my pain was a job for Connie.

"All I ever did was try to love him, and I did everything I could to make him happy and make him love me. I hate him to the very core of my being, and I wish I'd never met him — other than having my children. When I look at him I don't see the sweet person I met when I was 19, I see a demon. I look at him and I can see the evil behind his eyes. I know he is a despicable human being, and all he wants to do is hurt people. He only ever thinks of himself. He is a liar and a cheater and a manipulator. So, why in the hell do I feel like this?"

"How did you feel when you realized he had another woman back in the bedroom?"

"I was angry."

"What about it made you angry?"

"He was telling the kids he was still in love with me and he wanted me back. But he had another girl there with him. He lied to them. He made it seem like this was my fault."

"What else? Try to think of those feelings when you first realized she was there."

"Well, I felt sad."

"Okay. Why sadness?"

The fidget spinner from Connie's collection of toys on her side table whirled between my fingers.

"I think I was sad because I knew he was treating her better than he treated me. And I was his wife. It isn't fair. It made me really sad. Why does she deserve dates and dinners and gifts, but I don't? He is doing things with her he never did with me and it hurts."

"Do you believe you don't deserve those things?"

"Well, no! Of course not! I definitely deserve them."

"Okay. So how long do you think they have been dating each other?"

"I'm not sure, but I think a couple of months."

"And tell me, when you and he were dating for a couple of months, how was he treating you?"

My mind immediately went back to the happiest time of our relationship. I recalled the dates, the doting, the love letters, the attention, and affection. It was overwhelming and I felt very loved. The fidget spinner slowed and then came to a complete stop.

"Oh. I think I get it now."

"Well?" she asked.

"He's treating Hannah exactly how he used to treat me."

"So, what do you think it means for Hannah if they stay together for longer than a few months?"

"It means she is going to be disappointed."

Peeling back the layers of my emotions was so helpful. I wasn't going to heal through venting my frustrations and emotions alone. It was imperative that I got to the bottom of my issues in order to heal.

"Wow. This whole time I was looking at myself as the problem. Like 'why wasn't I good enough?'"

"Now you're getting it."

"It never was about me. It was always about Nick."

She nodded and smiled like a proud parent.

"Someone like Nick will do whatever he has to in order to get what he wants. He did it with you, and he will do it with her, too. Keep this in mind whenever you start to have those feelings creep up on you. Identify the feeling and then remember the truth about it. You will need to reject the lies he told you in your dysfunctional relationship in order to see the truth."

It sounded pretty easy, but I would learn it would be harder than I thought. It would take a lot of concentrated effort on my part. It would require me to be in touch with my feelings and not be afraid to face them. Healing these inner wounds was worth it, though. For my kids and for me.

CHAPTER 34

THE SEPARATION – YEAR 18, MONTH 1

Nick: *Hey, can I tell you something personal?*

Allie: *Sure.*

Nick: *So I ended it with Hannah. I didn't want the kids feeling like they were second best to her. Would you mind if I told them we broke up? They keep asking me about her. I feel bad for them always wondering about her.*

How do I respond to this? Did I want to be sympathetic to his breakup? Should I give him permission? Maybe I should just ignore it or tell him to ask his lawyer. My fingers typed up several different responses of which none satisfied me. I typed then deleted one after another as indecisiveness and fear paralyzed me. Instead of responding immediately, I decided to just think about it. My knee-jerk reaction was to be nice. My immediate instinct was to say yes. I had to squash it. I had to sit on this for some time before I replied, so I waited before responding.

Why is he asking my permission? He should be asking the lawyer. I don't believe him. He would never end it with Hannah. She was the perfect victim for him. Maybe she left him, but he didn't leave her. He is selfish. He doesn't put the kids first. He is using the children and playing on my sympathies so they don't "worry."

He doesn't want them feeling second best? That is easy to do without talking about Hannah. This is a lie. Everything he says is a lie. Why should I do anything for him to make things easier for him? If he's frustrated that the kids keep asking, he should be a parent and tell them to stop.

So many thoughts ran through my mind, so I decided to message Johnny for some advice.

Allie: *Do I need to reply to this text from Nick? What should I say? Why is he asking me this? Is this a set up?*

Johnny:
Didn't you tell me recently Hannah is supposed to be getting deposed by your lawyer in a week?

Allie: *Yeah. Why? It's just to scare her. Intimidation tactics, nothing more.*

Johnny: *Exactly. So think about it. If you were 23, dating a much older man with 3 kids and an ex-wife trying to bring you into the courtroom to testify, would you want to stick around?*

Allie: *LOL! No, definitely not!*

Johnny: *Nick knows this. He's trying to get you to back off and he's using the kids to appeal to your emotions. She is probably scared shitless. She will have to face you and your lawyer in the deposition and then appear in front of a judge. For what? For some guy she's been dating for a few months? Nah. She is not going to want to do THAT.*

Allie: *Son of a bitch. How did I not see that immediately?*

I was angry with myself for initially wanting to be nice to him. *Why is my base instinct to cater to his needs?* Again, he was attempting to manipulate me and lie about his relationship status while simultaneously using our children to get to me.

Johnny: *It's ok. You have to close the door for any further dialogue from him. You don't even want a 'thank you' from him. Make him question your response and worry about what you mean. He's playing games with you because that is how these kinds of people operate. You need to shut it down.*

Allie: *I don't know how.*

Johnny: *Say this - "LOL! Nice try Nick. See you both in court."*

Allie: *I can't say that!*

Johnny: *Why not? What are you afraid of?*

Allie: *I don't know! I just can't say that to him.*

Johnny: *I'm pretty sure you can and I'm 100% sure if you do, you will not regret it. You've got to trust me on this.*

I drew in a long breath of air, held it, and let it out slowly as I imagined what it might feel like to say something so bold to Nick.

Allie: *I'm so nervous.*

Johnny: *Of course you are! You've never talked to him like that before. He isn't going to know what to do and he probably won't even reply. He will wonder. Are you saying LOL because he supposedly ended it with her? Are you saying it because you are calling him on his lies? This is the most important part though. You are also telling him "I AM NOT AFRAID OF YOU." He's always held the power and now you are holding it. You do whatever you want Allie, but I'm telling you, if you do this, you win this battle.*

In my gut, I knew he was right. The next morning upon waking, I had a small window of courage. I typed the words on my screen, and I read them over and over.

Allie: *LOL! Nice try Nick. See you both in court.*

A small window of bravery opened up and knew it would close quickly. Before I could blink, I tapped Send.

Allie: *Johnny, I did it! I sent the text just how you suggested.*

Johnny: *I knew you could do it! I never doubted it once.*

Allie: *Thank you so much for helping me.*

The confidence Johnny had in me was exhilarating and calming at the same time.

My heart was beating fast and I was excited. I stared at my screen, and I waited for a reply from Nick. Then I waited for several days, and Nick never replied to the text. My confidence was raised exponentially, and it felt amazing.

Nick was flawed in many ways, but he continued to underestimate me. It wasn't until I stopped underestimating myself that I realized this. His focus remained on himself. Every choice he made, every word he spoke, and every text he typed was with Nick in mind. He wasn't able to see past his own reflection to notice what was going on behind him in the mirror.

He chose to abuse me because of my strength. He chose to abuse me because I had things he didn't, like empathy, joy, compassion, and love. It made perfect sense. If you play against the worst basketball team in the world and you win, who cares? But if you beat the best team in the world, you have something to hang your hat on. He couldn't feel good about himself by squashing an insignificant ant. It had to be a person better than him. I didn't look at myself as better than him. In fact, I looked at myself as inferior to him. We are taught not to do this. We are told time and time again that we are all equal. We are no better than anyone else. What I learned in my toxic marriage was that I most definitely am a better person than Nick, and I won't ever apologize for it.

CHAPTER 35

THE SEPARATION – YEAR 18, MONTH 2

"Mommy, when are we going to move into our own house?" Carter asked as we cuddled up in a fluffy blanket on Sasha's couch.

I didn't have an answer for him. We were in limbo for an undetermined length of time, and the kids had already been through the news of divorce and a move to a temporary home. Getting away from Nick was the first step, but, once I was able to leave, my highest priority became giving my children the stability they deserved after upsetting their little world.

"Oh, honey, I know you're anxious, but these things take some time," I explained.

"But what is taking so long? I just want us to have our own house."

"Well, my lawyer and I sent over some things to your dad and his lawyer about six weeks ago, and we still haven't heard anything back. My lawyer reached out to them several times, and we're just waiting on a reply."

"That's weird, because, when we asked Daddy, he told us you are holding up the divorce."

A fit of rage was clawing its way to the surface. Holding it at bay in front of my son was no small task. Nick blaming me was such a significant part of my marriage with him. He never took responsibility, even if his fault was lit up with neon lights. No one wants to or should be held accountable for something they didn't do. There weren't many things that infuriated me more than when Nick made false accusations against me. I wanted to scream. I wanted to break something while screaming. In my mind, I pictured Nick lying on the floor, and me stomping on his head. It made me feel better imagining it. I wondered if I'd feel worse if it actually happened. *What was so hard about accepting responsibility for his transgressions? Why couldn't he see how hurtful he was when he did this?*

Carter was just an innocent messenger of lies from his dad, so I kept my composure to avoid upsetting him. Nick purposefully twisted the truth to blame me for his procrastination. My kids would see it as me holding up their opportunity for stability.

"I believe your dad thinks I'm holding up the divorce," I said, "and I know this is complicated, but I won't lie to you. We made a request, and they will not respond to it. That request is not what your dad wants, and that's probably why he says I am holding up the divorce. To him, if I'd just give him what he wants, then everything would already be finalized."

"Well, what *do you* want Mommy?" he asked.

Carter has always been a sweet and caring little boy. His concern for me was sincere. Just eight years old and still full of empathy. He came to me without any judgment or accusations.

"I just want what's fair, baby. That's all. That's all I've ever wanted."

"You know what else? Daddy told me he thinks he's gonna win against you in court. He said everyone he knows agrees with him, and that you're gonna lose big time."

My blood was boiling. Nick knew this information was going to get back to me. His aim was to get a reaction, and I wasn't going to give him what he wanted. I decided I had to maintain my composure. Any reaction I exposed to Carter would definitely get back to Nick.

"Hmm, That's interesting," I said with as much monotone as I could muster. I recalled advice from Johnny. *Never let anyone see your hand. Keep a poker face. Don't let anyone know they've gotten to you.*

Claire trotted in the room and chimed into our conversation. She must have been eavesdropping.

"Dad told me you were really rude to him the other day when he told you he broke up with Hannah."

God is teaching me. I thought to myself. *Do not get angry.*

"Claire, how I communicate to your dad is nothing compared to what he did to me for nearly 20 years," I said calmly, staring directly into her eyes.

She was silent. She absorbed my words and stared back at me sympathetically.

"I'm sorry, baby. It's hard for me not to get upset."

"It's fine, Mom. I think you're doing a really great job. I'm proud of you and I know Dad wasn't treating you right."

My heart swelled in my chest. The daughter who said I ruined her life when I broke the divorce news was now seeing some truth. A thick knot formed at the back of my throat.

"Thank you."

"You know, Dad isn't nice to me either. He lets Lleyton get away with everything and babies Carter. He punishes me if I disagree with him or do anything he doesn't like."

"I'm sorry you have to deal with that, sweetheart. I fear some of his anger towards me might be taken out on you."

"Yeah, he always says, 'that's inappropriate Claire,' and 'don't argue with me.'"

"How do you handle that?"

"Well, if I ask him questions or disagree, he just tells me he's the dad and he makes the rules."

Nick never tolerated being disrespected by anyone. He didn't tolerate being challenged either. Pretty much anything that he didn't approve of was shot down immediately and it didn't matter who was on the receiving end, even if it were his children.

"See you both in court." I thought, reminiscing to the epic instance when I stood up to Nick in a way I never had before. It made me smile. Surely, it was an unpleasant surprise to Nick, and he thought I was going to buy his lies and give him exactly what he wanted as usual. He was wrong. Not only was he wrong; he was sulking. He had to run and tell his friends and family and even his children that I was rude to him in a text. My brain oozed with

sarcasm as I considered his whining. *God Nick, you're so pathetic. So annoying. Poor Nick. Nobody ever stood up to you before. Everyone eats your shit, but I refuse. Oh, and Nick? To top it off, I served your own shit right back to you on a silver platter. Poor, pitiful, Nick. So mistreated. How will you ever survive such a nasty text from me?* I laughed to myself and rolled my eyes. *He can't even tolerate a menial text laced in passive aggressive humor. Compared to everything I tolerated from him over the years, I'm a fucking fairy godmother.*

CHAPTER 36

THE SEPARATION – YEAR 18, MONTH 3

"Mommy, Dad went skydiving!" My oldest daughter boasted proudly one hot day in June as she hopped into the front seat. Her soccer bag flung onto the floorboard beneath her feet and her chestnut colored eyes flashed with excitement. The younger two hopped into the back, preoccupied with arguing over whose turn it was to hold the slime.

"Really," I stated.

With as much disinterest as I could muster, I focused on the backup camera as I put the SUV into reverse.

"Yes! Isn't that so awesome?!" She bounced in her seat, and her beautiful, dimpled smile had my focus. She's always wanted to fly. Three years in a row, she asked Santa for a flying broomstick like the ones in the Harry Potter novels.

I tried to channel my best thespian face to hide the plethora of emotions welling up inside me. I could feel the anger building from my toes towards my head. I took a deep breath, pulled my mirrored sunglasses down over my eyes, and gave her a forced tight lip smile.

"Yes, that's really awesome." But silently I was seething. *Too bad his parachute didn't fail.* Thoughts entered my mind of him falling toward Earth, fumbling unsuccessfully with his parachute release until he splattered on the ground - Dead.

"Can I go, too? Dad said it's up to you, but he said I could go when he takes us to Mexico next week on vacation. You don't even have to be eighteen there!"

So, there it was – The opportunity for me to squash her dream. He knew full well I was never going to agree to allow our barely twelve year-old daughter to flop out of some rickety airplane at ten-thousand feet in the air. Nick did this on purpose. He was making me the bad guy.

"Absolutely not." I blurted out before I could soften my words.

"Mom! Please?!" She begged.

"I really want to, and I won't have to wait 'til I'm 18!"

"No, baby. I'm not going to agree to that. There's a reason the law is eighteen here in America. It's too dangerous and my answer is no."

Nick tried his best behind my back to make my life as difficult as he could. Outwardly, he would tell me he wanted things to be as easy and nice as possible. He'd say he wanted things to be fair and for us to get through this as quickly as possible. He was saying everything he knew I wanted to hear, but inwardly, he was doing the opposite. He didn't want things to be easy and nice for me, he only wanted me not to resist him.

"You are so mean!" she yelled, tears welling in her eyes.

"Claire, I'm sorry, I just can't agree to let you skydive in Mexico."

"If you hadn't divorced Dad, he would make you let me go!"

The scream in her voice pierced my heart. I swallowed a lump in my throat to keep tears from falling. The guilt breaking up our home was overwhelming. My children didn't know why I left. I didn't want them to hate their father for what he had done to me. Every time they fired a bullet at me, I took it. Every time they told me they hated me for divorcing him, I took it. Every time their pain was too much to bear, I let them blame me. One day, they might know the truth. Either they will learn it for themselves as victims of their own father's abuse, or they will hear it from me when they are older. As for now, they need to be children. If asked, I promised them I'd be truthful. But I'd never go out of my way to alienate their father from their lives.

"Don't speak to me that way, Claire," I said as calmly as I could.

Bearing the guilt for leaving the marriage, navigating the legal processes involved in a complex divorce, and learning how to heal from years of emotional trauma was an immense weight on me. It seemed everything was happening at once. The overwhelming anxiety that plagued me led to loss of clarity, mistakes, and worry. I wasn't sure if I was equipped to handle the mounting stress and difficulties. *I can't do this.*

Nick was making irrational and unreasonable requests through his lawyer, but, in public, was smiling and acting like we were old friends. My heart was torn into pieces from the hurt I was causing my babies. Complex-PTSD, dysfunctional behaviors, and negative self-talk were just a few of the internal battles I fought every day. I was sinking naked in a thick swamp with venomous snakes and alligators beneath my feet and no dry land in sight. Trudging through the swamp was exhausting. In my weakness, I was beginning to sink deeper.

When the kids went to Nick's, I laid in bed in a deep depression. This was a different feeling than I'd ever had before. I slept, wept, and got up occasionally to use the bathroom. Nothing interested me. Not friends, not TV, not food, nothing. My stomach was so queasy I could barely keep water down. My face found a soft place in my tear-soaked pillow and stayed there for three solid days. My struggle was between wanting to go back to Nick to erase my emotional torment and knowing that, if I went back, I would retreat into his cage where I swore I'd never go back to. The alluring urge to return to a man I despised disoriented me. *How much easier would it be to just call all of this off? How much happier would my children be? I could go right back to my old life and never have to deal with this again. No more lawyers, no more fighting, no more guilt. Nick would be nice to me, I think, at least for a while. This is too hard. This is impossible. I should go home.*

As I laid there, I glanced across the room at the framed photo of my three, beautiful, tender-hearted children. Studying their smiling faces, I remembered why I started:

to save myself and protect my sweet little children. I couldn't give up on myself, and I couldn't give up on them. They deserved more from me. I had to keep fighting. I needed to be a warrior for them.

I spent some time reflecting and decided to snap out of it. I dragged myself out of bed and into the bathroom. A sad and defeated Allie reflected back at me in the mirror. Oily brown locks were matted to my head and smears of mascara covered my eyes. I told myself aloud:

You do not miss him, you never did. He was never the love of your life. You miss what he pretended to be at the beginning. You miss what could have been even though it never would have been. This is because he was a fraud. He lied to you for years and tricked you into believing he was good. But he was never good. It was all a big, elaborate magic trick. And you fell for it. You are damaged because of him. But you are repairable. You will heal from this. Don't give up, whatever you do, don't you ever fucking give up.

CHAPTER 37

THE SEPARATION – YEAR 18, MONTH 4

Since leaving Nick and learning about how to deal with emotional abusers, I tried desperately to not engage. I promised myself I would not engage with drama from him, his family, or his friends. People who were not on my side would simply have to be ignored. In my past, I'd always tried to take the high road. Too often this behavior allowed others to mistreat and manipulate me. These types of actions got me into trouble, more than once.

Months had gone by without me hearing from anyone in Nick's family. Generally, they all ignored me in public. This was perfectly acceptable to me. I took this as a clear message they were not interested in me and did not care about me whatsoever. I steered clear of them and they reciprocated. The surprise came when Nick's brother, Adam, sent me an unexpected message.

Adam: *Well, Nick and Jenny don't know I'm sending you this. They'd both try to stop me, but when do I ever listen to anyone? I don't really know how to say this, but here goes. Nobody is perfect. You know this. God knows I have my flaws and I'm just glad Jenny points them out so I can try to be better. I think people should take a long hard look at how much they need to try and change. Listen, I'm not trying to back you into a corner. I just want to make sure this divorce thing is really what you want. Some of my friends are divorced and still say they think they could've saved it. I'm sure this is hard and I can't imagine how you're feeling. I bet you have all kinds of emotions, good and bad. I'm willing to talk if you have second thoughts. If you have any worries about ruining things with the kids and such a long marriage, we can talk. Jenny doesn't want to upset you, but it's killing her. I love your kids and hate this situation for everyone. If this makes you mad, I get it. I'm adult enough to know I'm not perfect and would change things if I knew it would make my wife and kids' lives better. Everyone has good in them. Remember that.*

Adam and I were family. We had memories together. He was my brother-in-law. It must have taken some courage for him to type his text. I realized that my decision to leave wasn't just affecting me and my kids and Nick. It spawned out into the family as well as into friend groups. Though I promised not to engage, I felt I could be the bigger person and send a nice, simple reply. I never expected what would come next.

Allie: *Hi Adam. I really appreciate your concern. I know this is hard on everyone and hard to understand. Please just know, I'm happier than I've ever been before. Thanks for being a loving uncle to my kids.*

That was it. That's all I wrote. I sincerely figured this was a good reply. It was short and sweet and to the point. I didn't address any of his feelings and didn't piggyback on any of his blatant and translucent accusations. Adam was a lot like Nick.

Replying was a mistake. I should have known better. I opened the door to more accusations and abuse from Nick's brother by my fear of appearing to be "rude." I regretted it the instant I received Adam's reply.

Adam: *Is that true? I don't know. Take some time to really think about what I'm gonna say. Why are you mean to Nick and our family if you are "so happy" as you claim? Happy people aren't mean. You should be the bigger person and be nice. You need to act like this is serious and realize this is killing everyone. It's not all about you. When you ignore my mom and Nick, it doesn't help. All I care about is my wife. She is hurting. She's in a horrible spot. She's at peace with you all not saving your marriage. But she is not ready to act like nothing's wrong and ignore everything. You need to help us find a way to learn to adjust to this. Hopefully someday things will be normal but that is not today. Not even close. Good luck.*

Adam had triggered me. Not once, but twice! This was my fault. This could have been avoided had I just not replied. It wasn't going to happen again, so I closed the message out and decided not to afford him another response from me.

Over several days, I mulled over what Adam had said and I finally came to the conclusion that it wasn't something I wanted taking up anymore of my mental energy.

The small town I live in forced me to run into people even if I preferred not to. My in-law's children go to school with mine. We all frequented the same stores. I was bound to encounter many people whom I wish I'd never have to see for the rest of my life.

One afternoon following Carter's soccer game, I was tossing some soccer chairs into my trunk when someone approached me from behind. I turned to see who it was. Adam was a few feet away and close enough to see emotions on my face. *Don't show emotion. Keep a straight face.* I dropped my arms to my sides and planted my feet into the bumpy gravel beneath my flip-flops. He stopped and looked at me, almost as if he were trying to say something. I concentrated on keeping a stoic expression on my face, waiting nervously to see if he would come closer and speak to me.

Adam turned away and funneled into the parking lot with other soccer parents who were packing up their vehicles to leave. As I watched, he smiled and made upbeat conversation with acquaintances. So similar to Nick, he was. He put his best face on in front of others, but I knew the truth about him. Jenny and I were close, and she shared intimate details of their life together. We cried on each other's shoulders. We bitched and complained about our husbands' behaviors and similarities, so critical and so hypocritical. I'd witnessed first-hand Adam mistreating Jenny and even his own mother. Behind closed doors, the true face was revealed, just like it was with Nick.

I wanted to scream at him from across the parking lot. *Asshole!* Maybe part of my rage was because of Nick, but it was also because I knew he would continue to mistreat my friend and my sweet sister by marriage. In my mind, I imagined getting in front of him and saying all the truths he would never admit.

You are a small excuse for a man with a fat wallet. Your so-called friends only stay because you entertain them with your big house, your pool, and your parties. They don't care about you. If you took all of that away from them, there's nothing left to make them stay. Do you actually think they would stay by your side if you lost everything? There's nothing about you that makes them want to stay. You BUY your friends through hosting parties you pay for. You treat your wife, your kids, your so-called friends, and your family as if they were inferior to you. And you can because they let you. They are willing to accept your abuse in exchange for an association with fake elitism and free handouts. What's pathetic is that you don't even have the money. You are broke. You are upside down on credit and headed further in debt. It's one thing to buy friends if you have money, and it's another thing to do it when you are in debt. You pretend to have money, but you don't. You rob Peter to pay Paul just trying to keep your head above water. They don't love you. They don't even like you. They tolerate you for their own selfish desires. But I won't. I won't give you the time of day ever again. I can see right through you, because you lack human substance. I refuse to be associated with that. If you lack humanity, what is left?

Saying these words with my mouth or in writing wouldn't do me any good. People like Adam take these types of confrontations and use them as fuel to retaliate. They refuse to see their flaws and, even if pointed out, they shirk responsibility. Revealing my opinions of Adam would put me in the exact position he wanted, engaged in conflict.

As much as I would have loved to call him out on all the lies he tries to hide, I knew it wasn't worth it. Stirring the pot, being argumentative and aggressive just wasn't going to matter. I shut my mouth and the trunk and made my way around to the driver's side of my vehicle. I looked back in his direction, feeling nothing but pity.

CHAPTER 38

THE SEPARATION - YEAR 18, MONTH 5

During the healing process, I found out all kinds of things about myself. After leaving Nick, my trust in other people was shattered, or at least I thought so. I was skeptical of everyone. My family and friends whom I had trusted for years before had new microscopes on them. Because I had trusted Nick for so long and realized how I had been lied to and manipulated, trust in pretty much everyone flew out the window. How could anyone be trusted? I had built a solid, steel wall around my heart and emotions. I was afraid to go back into Nick's cage. Kicking and screaming or being dragged against my will was the only way it would ever happen. Never would I ever willfully enter that prison again.

"I just don't trust anyone. I'm peering at them with suspicious eyes. I'm hanging on every word wondering if it is intended to control me. I don't want to be this way. I don't want to teach my kids to be this way either, but I don't know how NOT to do it. I feel like I am torn between two Allies. One is saying 'trust your gut, they are trying to control you,' while the other is saying, 'this is not logical, they've never given you any reason to not trust. I don't know how to fix this.'"

The inner conflict with which I battled was evident to my therapist, and I emptied my fears into her cozy, little office. With desperation, I pleaded for help. All I wanted to do was fix the brokenness I felt and be whole again. She looked at me with compassion and tenderness.

"So, I understand what you're saying and the reason you feel this way is because you have a form of PTSD. It has become instinctual for you not to trust. It's a coping strategy now. But what you don't realize is it's not the external factors or people you don't trust, it's yourself."

We stared at each other for a minute as I tried to digest what I'd heard. She sensed my skepticism.

"See, you are looking at the old Allie. When you think of her, what do you think?"

"She was stupid. She was weak. I feel sorry for her."

"But she wasn't those things. She was abused. She was treated badly, and she was tricked. She trusted her husband who was supposed to love her, and she didn't know it was the wrong thing to do. So, now, if you are the old Allie looking at the new Allie, what does she see?"

"Old Allie is excited! She is envious of new Allie and wants to be just like her. She is proud of her."

"Now, do you see how far you've come?"

Reflecting on Connie's questions and seeing my old and new selves was enlightening. Sadness and pride intermingled in my mind like chocolate and vanilla swirl ice cream.

"Yes! I do. But I don't know how to trust myself like you say."

"Does old Allie trust new Allie?"

I kicked off my shoes and pulled my feet up underneath me on the couch and hugged my shins.

"Yes. She does."

"Then, why don't you?"

I let out a heavy sigh and laid my forehead on my knees, exasperated.

"I don't know. But I know I should. And I really want to."

"Yes, you should. You need to trust yourself knowing you will not allow someone to take advantage of you again. You can trust people until they give you a reason not to trust them. Do you understand?"

I nodded, soaking in her wisdom but still uneasy about the feeling it gave me.

"Yeah, I do. I think I can do that. It's scary, but unless someone gives me a reason not to trust them, I can try."

"Right, and, at that point, if someone gives you a reason not to trust them, then that is when you make a decision on how you would like to handle the relationship. You need to trust yourself. You know you aren't going to let something else bad happen to you like it did before. You are aware of the red flags now. You know what is unacceptable behavior."

The clarity I felt was like someone had just spring cleaned my mind. I was amazed at my ignorance. I was placing all of my trust on external influences where I needed to simply trust myself. I was jaded. My former self was not who I wanted to be. She was weak. The new Allie needed to avoid regressing back to a weakened state. She needed to be strong and skeptical of everyone.

"Wow," I mused.

The epiphany slammed into me like a homerun crack of a wooden baseball bat.

"Allie, you don't trust yourself because you have not yet accepted who you are. You are not the same person you used to be. You are no longer a victim. You are a survivor now. You made changes to your life and to who you are. You should wholeheartedly trust yourself. You saved Allie. You saved yourself."

Immense pride welled up within my chest. Heat filled my hazel eyes as warm tears of happiness blurred my vision. I blinked gently to keep them from rolling down my face. Connie leaned out of her chair and handed me a tissue.

"You need to accept this about yourself, Allie. Do you hear the power in those words? You saved yourself."

I repeated the words in my mind. *I saved myself.* And then I couldn't keep the happy tears from flowing. And I didn't want to anyway. This was my joy and I earned it.

CHAPTER 39

The Separation - Year 18, Month 6

"How are you feeling today?" Connie asked.

"I'm fucking pissed off!"

"What happened?"

"He just won't stop. I've been physically away from him for over a year, but he keeps lying and manipulating the kids. He continually tries to manipulate and lie to me. Luckily, I can figure it out pretty fast. It just makes me furious. I don't want to feel like this, because I feel like, when I get angry, he's winning. I want to forgive him for myself to heal but I can't."

"Okay, so what is the feeling you get when he tries to lie and manipulate you?"

I shut my eyes tightly, taking myself back to the last email he sent me. It was littered with lies, selfishness, and manipulation. Anger was the only thing I could feel.

"What is the very first emotion you feel when he lies and tries to manipulate you?"

I paused, flipping through the feelings of my emotional filing cabinet. *Which one is it?*

"It's anger."

"Let's try to dig a little deeper."

Connie was helping me to peel back the layers to get to the heart of what the issue was. I couldn't see it, because the anger had built up so much, hiding the real problem. I gave her examples of recent text messages he'd sent and dissected them while venting my frustrations. She listened intently, nodding and taking in everything I was saying. She urged me to keep talking and finally, through much discussion, I spit it out.

"It's fear. It's not anger. I'm afraid he's going to trick me again like he did in the marriage. I'm afraid he's going to hurt me again with his lies and manipulation."

"Okay, let me ask you something else." I nodded, anxious for her to help me get the bottom of this. "Since you left, have there been any times you were able to recognize what he was doing, and you were able to protect yourself from him?"

"Yes!" I said, proudly. "Many times: in mediation, in court, with custody stuff, with texts. A lot of times, now that I think about it."

"Now we are getting somewhere. You actually have specific examples of times where you have been successful at protecting yourself from Nick. You have proof and evidence of your ability to do that."

My eyes widened. It was clear now to me what was causing my anger.

"I have all the skills I need to protect myself from Nick!" I shouted, bouncing on the leather seat with excitement. My eyes welled with tears as I realized how easy this will be and how easy it could have been all along.

"That's right. You are fully capable of protecting yourself against him, so you don't have to be afraid. Recognize the feeling immediately, take a second, then remind yourself of that every time you come in contact with him. You see, your anger was the secondary emotion and fear was the first. When you're no longer afraid, you take back control."

An instant feeling of relief rushed over me like an icy breeze on a sweltering summer day. Finally, it made sense. The sense of power was invigorating. By identifying the root emotions, I was able to take back control and be freed from my own bondage.

"One other thing. I want you to think about if there's anything Nick has taught you or if there's anything about this you can be grateful for. This should also help in your healing process."

She was going to get resistance on this task. Admitting Nick did anything positive in my life made me feel gross. In my mind, he didn't deserve any credit for anything. I still wished he were dead because he made parts of my life hard. If he would just vanish, I wouldn't have to deal with this anymore. If he was just gone, like a wisp of smoke, I could feel normal and happy again. How on earth was I going to be grateful for anything when it came to Nick?

One thing I knew for certain was my hate for Nick had been holding me back so long and I couldn't deny it. Forgiving him for what he did was so difficult because he continued to repeat the same offenses. Even after fake apologies, he kept hurting me. It's one thing to forgive someone who admits wrongdoings and makes changes. It's completely different to forgive someone who never changes. I didn't know how to do this. I wanted to forgive his transgressions so badly so that I could heal. Not for him, but for me. I needed to forgive him so I could move on.

It would take some practice, but, with fear and anger no longer looming over me like a dark cloud, the path to my healing through forgiveness was becoming easier to do. I didn't want to be consumed with hatred.

When I got home after my session, I decided to write Nick a letter. I'd never send it to him. I just needed to get some mental clarity and I hoped this would help.

Nick,

I didn't include the 'dear' salutation, because you are no longer dear to me. One thing you are to me is a teacher. No matter how badly I wanted to launch you off the edge of a cliff after watching you deepthroat a cactus, I can't deny you are an ultimate educator. This was never your intention. It happened inadvertently. You made every valiant effort to chip away at my character. You tirelessly worked to slash and rip at my soul. When I was drowning in despair, I looked for your hand to pull me up and realized it was you who pushed me under. You were the hardest working teacher I ever had. You diligently persisted in disturbing the ground beneath my feet as I clawed and scraped to climb out of the pit of your persecution.

Confusion and denial constantly filled my thoughts as you toyed with my strings like a marionette. But still, I thank you. I am eternally grateful for what you put me through. I am overflowing with love and hope for my future only because of your hate. Your devious and evil ways permeated my every waking hour and have transformed me into a tower of strength. I can see for miles. I can see the evil in this world, and I am no longer afraid of it. I am no longer afraid of you.

You taught me that love with conditions isn't actually love at all. I learned there's no room for fear in a relationship and especially not a marriage. I know giving is a virtue, but it's also a two-way street. My voice is strong now, and I can say no and respect myself and demand respect from others. I've realized unless I love myself first, I truly believe no one else will ever be able to love me either.

You taught me all those things, Nick. If I had it to do over again, I would still experience this trauma from you because it changed me. You carved away pieces of me, and when I put them back together, I was a better version of myself. I would recognize this bullshit a hell of a lot sooner if I had to experience it again. You stole so much of my life from me. You stole parts of my personality, and you stole my emotions. You are a reprehensible thief, taking as you please from my giving heart. You will do this again to someone new, and I will watch from a distance as you get away with your terrible crimes. I know the truth of who and what you are, and I also know the truth of who I am. I am healing, and I am a survivor, and you will never have control over me again.

Where I used to lean on you, I now lean on God and myself. Where I used to consult you, I make my own decisions. Where I used to worry, I now have faith. Where I used to trust you, I now trust myself.

You no longer have any influence on me. Not because you stopped trying, but because I stopped allowing you to. Where one door closes, another shall be opened. I opened my own door to the cage you held me in, and I transformed into a brilliant phoenix leaving a trail of fire behind me for everyone to see. So, thank you Poisonous Professor. Thank you for what you made me endure. Without it, I'd be standing still, never taking a step away from fear. Never realizing my true potential and never knowing who I would become.

Allie

I came to realize that I never wanted to kill Nick because of my hate towards him. Not in the literal sense. I just wanted to remove what was hurting me, and I didn't know how. He was the source of my pain, and he was the reason for my despair. The power I gave to him was mine and I didn't know how to get it back. On the surface, I thought the only way to rid my life of pain was to physically destroy him so he could never hurt me again. However, the massive mistake in my thinking was that he actually had no power over me to begin with.

The one who I really wanted to destroy was the weak and timid version of myself that was holding me back. The one who needed to go was the woman who bowed to this evil monster. The pathetic, weak person who ignored her good instincts and disregarded all the red flags flying in her face needed to die. That person was holding me back. She had to die.

Now she is dead. Not by Nick's hand, but by my own. The only way I could allow the best version of myself to emerge was to destroy her forever. I look back at her with sadness, but also with gratitude. Though she isn't who I wanted her to be, she was also my hero. She was the survivor in me with the stubborn refusal to give up. Without her, I would have never discovered my true strength. She was resilient and loving, and she never conceded to the evil that tried to destroy her. She fought valiantly for the life of whom she knew I could become. She would be a sacrificial lamb for the emergence of a new me. After I killed her, I admired her strength, laid her down gently, and kissed her goodbye forever. I thanked her for what she did for me and for fighting so hard for the person I am now.

It's true that during the worst part of my abuse, I yearned for an easy way out. But the easy way out wasn't going to help me grow. We must always choose courage over comfort. Nick's death in my fantasies was the simplest solution to a problem that would never go away unless I learned and changed. I would remain the same shell of a person I always was in another destructive relationship with someone else, just like Nick. Trekking and conquering this mountain was not only necessary for my growth, it was also critical for the survival of my soul.

We finalized the divorce after two grueling years of legal battles and Nick is alive and breathing today. He only ever died in my imagination. He's moved on to another unsuspecting woman and the cycle continues. No matter how much I want to warn and save all of the Hannahs of the world, they have their own swamps to trudge through.

They have their own mountains to climb. They even have their own revolting personas to assassinate.

Yes, we are survivors, but we are also warriors. Your story is not mine and my story is not yours, but each one is just as important as the other. The only way we can triumph over this type of evil is to shout our stories from the cliffs we scale so that other victims will always know the way.

ENJOY THIS BOOK?

YOU CAN MAKE A BIG DIFFERENCE!

I am so grateful for my committed and loyal readers! Your reviews are one of the best thank-yous I can receive.

Reviews are the most powerful tool I have as an author when it comes to bringing my books to the attention of other readers.

If you enjoyed this book, I would be very grateful if you could spend just five minutes leaving a review (it can be as short as you like) on the book's Amazon page.

CONNECT

AND DISCOVER HELPFUL RESOURCES

One of the best parts of being a writer is connecting with my readers. I'm also passionate about expanding awareness of this type of covert and rampant abuse as well as inspiring those who have been victimized in this way.

Connect with me and get started with two free electronic infographics - *8 Signs you might be Emotionally Abused & how to Exit Safely* and *5 Easy Exercises to Rewire your Brain for Better Self Worth* by signing up for my mailing list at:

www.whentearsleavescars.com

ADDITIONAL RESOURCES

Allison K. Dagney
Certified Rapid Reprogramming™ Coach
www.whentearsleavescars.com

Shannon Thomas, LCSW & author of *Healing from Hidden Abuse* and *Exposing Financial Abuse: When Money is a Weapon*
www.shannonthomas.com

ABOUT THE AUTHOR

Allison K. Dagney lives in the midwest of the United States with her three children and their beloved rescue dog. She enjoys spending time with her children, playing in nature, helping others as a Thought Work Coach, and of course writing. Allison never aspired to be an author, but her love of writing paired with an inspirational story, was the perfect recipe to expose hidden, emotional abuse.

Her goal is to expand awareness of this covert and rampant type of abuse as well as to give inspiration to those who have been victimized in this way. Ultimately, Allison wishes to help victims gain needed strength to escape, while helping outsiders gain a better understanding of hidden abuse.

ACKNOWLEDGEMENTS

Even through a storm, there is always something to be thankful for. Throughout the process of writing this memoir, there have been many people who have supported, encouraged, and loved me. Each and every one of them deserves my thanks.

God, first and foremost, thank you. All of the gifts and opportunities that have been presented to me come from the Lord. All praise and glory go to my Heavenly Father who protected me through my abuse and uplifted me to rise above it.

My amazing significant other and life partner, thank you for supporting me and encouraging me during this process. Thank you for pushing me to be the very best version of myself and loving me unconditionally.

To my amazing mom who was there for me during the writing of this book. Your faith in my dream means more to me than you'll ever know.

My good friends and wonderful readers—WG, JS, CL, SF, TB and KN—thank you for being my biggest cheerleaders, constructive coaches, and supportive sounding boards. Each one of you helped me as I walked the path to becoming an author.

Heather, my formatting editor, cover-designer, and coach. Your creative artistry brought my vision to life! Your experience and knowledge has been invaluable to my journey as a writer.

Blanche Gaynor, my line editor, thanks for your impeccable eye for detail and assisting me in presenting a beautifully polished piece of work.

Jennifer Blanchard, my developmental editor, your review of my manuscript was illuminating. It was the boost I needed to make the leap from writer to author. Your expertise is priceless.

To my final editor, Taylor Winkleski, whose impeccable eye for detail propelled this manuscript forward. Thank you for your enthusiastic support of my book and keen editing skills.

Finally, to all survivors of domestic abuse, some whom I've known personally and others whose paths intersected with mine. You were the inspiration for me to keep going to get this book to print. You were the reason I started and never quit. Thank you.

Printed in Great Britain
by Amazon

84798078R00164